MAKING GOOD

MAKING GOOD

The Inspiring Story of a Serial Entrepreneur, Maverick and Restaurateur

TONY ALLAN

CAPSTONE

First published 2006 by

Capstone Publishing Limited (a Wiley Company)
The Atrium
Southern Gate
Chichester
West Sussex
PO19 8SQ
www.wileyeurope.com

Email (for orders and customer service enquires): cs-books@wiley.co.uk

Other Wiley Editorial Offices

John Wiley & Sons Inc., 111 River Street, Hoboken, NJ 07030, USA
Jossey-Bass, 989 Market Street, San Francisco, CA 94103-1741, USA
Wiley-VCH Verlag GmbH, Boschstr. 12, D-69469 Weinheim, Germany
John Wiley & Sons Australia Ltd, 42 McDougall Street, Milton, Queensland 4064, Australia
John Wiley & Sons (Asia) Pte Ltd, 2 Clementi Loop #02-01, Jin Xing Distripark, Singapore 129809
John Wiley & Sons Canada Ltd, 22 Worcester Road, Etobicoke, Ontario, Canada M9W 1L1

Wiley also publishes its books in a variety of electronic formats. Some content that appears in print may not be available in electronic books.

British Library Cataloging in Publication Data
A catalogue record for this book is available from the British Library

ISBN 13: 978-1-84112-631-9
ISBN 10: 1-84112-631-4

Typeset in Photina MT 11/16pt by Sparks (www.sparks.co.uk)
Printed and bound in Great Britain by TJ International Ltd, Padstow, Cornwall

This book is printed on acid-free paper responsibly manufactured from sustainable forestry in which at least two trees are planted for each one used for paper production.

Substantial discounts on bulk quantities of Capstone Books are available to corporations, profes- sional associations and other organizations. For details telephone John Wiley & Sons on (+44) 1243-770441, fax (+44) 1243 770571 or email corporatedevelopment@wiley.co.uk

Contents

Acknowledgements

This book tells the story of success, but none of it could have been achieved without the loyal support of my family, friends and colleagues. Denys, my wife, has supported me from the very beginning, when I was just a chef without a job, as have my parents. In the restaurant industry Ronnie Truss, Christian Delteil and Giorgio Locatelli are among the most talented chefs I have ever met, and I am honoured to count them as friends. And the support of my mate Vinnie Jones through thick and thin has always been something I value. To them, and all the other talented people who appear in these pages, my sincerest thanks.

Dramatis Personae

Denys Allan – Tony's wife of twenty years.

Ronnie Truss – Tony's long-term partner in Cutty's fish wholesale business, and later in Bank.

Mark Allan – Tony's older brother, who joined him in the Cutty's business but later became a rival bidder for it.

Christian Delteil – head chef of Bank restaurant when Tony launched it, and now the managing director of Bank Restaurant Group.

Julian Wickham – noted architect and restaurant designer who designed many of Tony's restaurants, including Bank restaurant and its controversial glass chandelier.

Paul Gilligan – former property buyer for Pizza Express, hired by Tony Allan to be chief executive for Fish! plc before its administration.

Giorgio Locatelli – Italian chef who is one of Tony's closest friends. Together they did the *Tony & Giorgio* series for the BBC.

Marco Pierre White – celebrity chef who sued Tony for libel in a case settled out of court.

Michel Roux – influential celebrity chef who became a non-executive director of Fish!

Vinnie Jones – footballer-turned-film star who is a close personal friend of Tony through their mutual interest in game shooting.

Andrew Cohen – former owner of Betterware, Tony's current business partner.

Chapter One

The First Few Quid

I T WAS December, one o'clock in the morning and freezing cold, but the sweat was pouring off me. I could feel my heart pounding. It was pitch black up on the roof, but below me I could see the yellow sodium glow of the street lights and some-times a car going past. Every time you saw car headlights or any-thing, you would switch the torch off and you'd have to lay low for a bit, all the time a cold sweat running down inside your clothes. I was buzzing with it though. There was the pressure of worrying would my father find out, and the police as well – I was damn sure I didn't want to be caught – and I only had a limited time to do it in, so the adrenalin was really flowing. But I kept going. I had this target that I was going to do the lot – strip the whole roof of lead. And I'd set myself timespans over a period of months for the job. I would work it out: how long it takes me to get one section up and then try to work that out over days – all bearing in mind how often I could get out at night without being noticed. It was hard work though, trying to take lead flashings up. They were solid lead roof coverings, not just little bits of flashing round the side. My muscles were shaking with the effort, pulling the lead pieces back and roll-ing them up in strips.

I was fifteen then, and I'd already had a couple of little scams on the side going on. The lead thing got started one day when we were playing football in the playground at school. It was in the winter. It was wet and the football pitches were getting cut up, so we used to play in the playground with a tennis ball. I remember the ball went up on the roof, and I climbed up onto a portacabin and then onto the main roof. It was a flat roof, a big flat roof. It must have been have been a hundred feet by sixty feet; I looked at the covering of the roof and it was lead. While I was getting the ball down I actually used my fingers and just pulled back a bit and realized how easily it came off. That reminded me of something that had happened the summer before, when I first started working for my dad, who was a builder.

You got eight weeks off school for the holidays, and as soon as I was about fourteen years old I had to go to work with my dad through the summer. I had a girlfriend at the time, so I'd rather have seen her or gone out with my mates fishing but I had to go with my father. I was in the back of the van and he picked up some labourers from Eltham and we went on into Brixton, where he was converting a row of terraced houses into flats. He needed some building materials to start the job and I jumped in the front of the van with one of the men and we ended up near London Bridge – Druid Street it was. I saw this blackboard which said 'lead £30 a hundredweight, copper £75 a hundredweight'. So I asked the guy driving, 'What does that mean?' and he said, 'Well, you take lead in there and if it weighs over a hundredweight they give you that much money per hundredweight'.

That just stayed in the back of my mind, so when I saw all the lead on the school roof it got me thinking. I was at Hurstmere Secondary Modern School, Sidcup, in south London, which was an all-boys school that had quite a reputation for being a tough school. Right opposite was a famous acting college, Rosemount, where Gary Oldman and Anthony Andrews went. Then nearby was The Hollies, a children's care home. So I looked at all their roofs, and they all had lead on them. Well, I kept it to myself at first, but then I needed to be able to move the lead, so I got a bloke I knew who was 17 and worked in a fruit and veg shop – and he had a van, right. So I made this plan that if I stripped the roofs and stored the lead, then he could take it to the scrap dealer. And that was how it was: first I did the school, then I did the college, then I did The Hollies. Just stripped off all the lead. It took about six months, working three nights a week. For the first couple of months it was just me, but then my mate Paul joined in. After that we were developing the operation to the other two roofs, so we had to expand. I found a couple of guys and gave them a fiver a night to carry the lead to a hiding place for me, where I could get it picked up in the van later. It was quite a slick operation. I was probably making about £800 a week, and this was back in the 70s, in 1978.

It got to be a routine. I would go out with my girlfriend or go to the youth club and get in about ten o'clock at night. Then I would go to bed, but stay awake and wait for everybody to go to sleep, then jump out the back window. I would get started on the roof at about one o'clock in the morning, work 'til four, then sneak back in and my mum would wake me up on her way to work. I'd go off to school, or not as the case may be, do whatever I was doing, and then get ready for the next night. And the strange thing was: I could do it. When I got back in the early hours I would be exhilarated, buzzing still, but I always seemed to calm down quite quickly and then I'd crash out and go to sleep and be fine on just three or four hours' sleep. It's a habit that has stuck with me, and I suppose it's been pretty useful for someone working in the restaurant trade, with the late hours you keep in the kitchen.

It did get to me though, that sense of danger. I was very, very concerned, scared that is, about what might happen if my father found out. Because my dad had always said if you ever bring the police to my door, that's your lot. Not that I ever got to find out exactly what 'your lot' was. The end came when my mate Paul and I were just finishing the last bit of the children's home. By this time I must have saved up about fifteen grand, and that's a phenomenal amount of money for a teenage kid in the 70s. But my father had no idea this was going on, none of the family did. I had put a little bit of the money in a post office account, but the rest of it I had in cash. I actually had it hidden in a tin under my bed. But it couldn't go on. It wasn't Paul and I who were caught but the other two guys that I was paying to carry the lead across to the hiding place. Their job was to take the lead over the road and stick it in the back garden of this house we knew about whose owners had just moved to America, so it was empty while it was waiting to be rented out. The two guys were stopped by the police as they were carrying the lead across the road and taken to the police station – which was quite funny really because one of them, Craig, his dad was the Chief Inspector of Greenwich nick!

Anyway I waited until it was all clear and went back home as usual. But the next morning I went into school and at the gates I could see two police cars with their flashing lights on and the police talking to the headmaster. So I just said to Paul, 'Look, that's for us two' and he said he wasn't bothered. I told him, 'My old man's gonna kill me', but Paul said, 'Well my old man's not gonna kill me'. His mum and dad had split up. He'd probably not even get a rap on the knuckles. Because his mum was on her own and bringing him up – she probably would have laughed at it, but I knew my dad would absolutely fucking murder me, and I thought I have to get out of here. So I asked Paul did he want to come. We went back to my house and got a rucksack, a sleeping bag, and a load of canned food. I nicked a blowtorch out of the back of one my dad's vans, grabbed a wadge of money, and we jumped on the number 51 bus which went to Green Street Green in North Kent. We ended up a bit further out into the countryside, in Cudham, and we spent our first night on the run in a haystack. We had about £500 on us, quite a lot for those days. So there we were sleeping in this bloody uncomfortable haystack. And strangely enough that first night they very nearly found us. We saw the torches, which were my dad and my brother, but they went right past us.

Then the next day we found this clearing in the woods with log cabins – it turned out to be a camping site for Girl Guides. We broke into one of the log cabins and discovered hammocks in there, a little stove and everything. We had all we needed, so we set up camp in there. We even got a job down the road cutting down Christmas trees for the local farmer. By this time I am pretty sure we were registered as missing persons but to us it was just a big adventure. We had been gone about five or six days when I went down into the next village, which was Downe, not far from Biggin Hill, because I wanted to phone my girlfriend to tell her not to worry. It was a phone box and my two pence pieces were running out so I gave her the number of the box for her to call me back. She told her parents though and they phoned the police and before we could get back to the camp we started hearing the sirens.

We were beside a big church with a churchyard with yew trees. Quickly we climbed up into one of the yew trees. It's extraordinary, if you climb up inside a yew tree, when you get to the top it's like a bed, a platform. There we were at the top of the yew tree looking down at this serious operation to find these two missing guys, who were fourteen, fifteen years old. They still didn't get us though, and we stayed out another night. By the morning I was worrying about my mum and I had to phone her. I said, 'I'm fine, but I'm not coming home.' She said 'Come home. Look, your dad's not going do anything, he just wants to see you back.' Eventually my girlfriend's father come and took us to the police station where all we got was a slap on the wrist and a caution.

But we'd been a pretty successful pair of runaways. Paul and I had always been a great team together. Even from the age of twelve we used to spend a lot of weekends camping out to go bird watching at places like Cliffe marshes out in Dickens country in North East Kent. My dad had even told the police, 'You can put them down as missing persons, but that's the best survival team you're ever going to come across. Those lads go off for weekends with just a sheepskin coat and a pair of binoculars, and they've always come back before.'

The thing was, I'm not sure how much they connected us running away with the other two lads being picked up for the lead. They probably suspected, but they never pinned the lead job on me or anything like that. But why did I do it? I'm not even sure really, why I nicked all that lead. We were comfortably off: Dad, Mum and the three of us kids, living in Sidcup. It's not as if we children went short. Obviously at the time it was the challenge of actually doing it that meant more to me than anything else – it was exciting, a big adventure for a kid. But behind that one of the things driving me was what was happening with my brother, Mark.

Mark is a year and a half older than me, but you couldn't have two more different brothers. He was an academic at school, but also he was potentially a fabulous footballer. He was in the England Youth Team and he was offered premiership trials – division one it was then – yet he chose to go to university rather than sign for the top clubs that wanted him. I suppose for our dad it was all very much of a quandary. It must have been new territory for someone in the building game trying to advise a son with umpteen O levels and on his way to four A levels. All I remember Mark doing was studying. Studying, and playing football. In the end he chose to go to Ulster University in Northern Ireland. I'm sure my father must have talked to him about the money. Even then the money in football was astronomical compared with the average wage, and Mark could have had a pretty decent living. He would have made it as a professional footballer without any shadow of a doubt. My brother was certainly the golden boy – excellent academically and a brilliant sportsman, but he has never had one ounce of common sense.

He would come home from university and I know he was under pressure, trying to get his degree in Ulster with the troubles going on all round him, but even so I felt that he could have shown more consideration for our parents. I didn't want to be repeating the situation of continually asking my parents for money, so the lead money became a way to take the pressure off. It was a good feeling to know in the back of my mind that they weren't going to have to give me anything. When I was making that money, I kept it to myself. I never asked my parents for anything. From the age of fifteen I didn't ask them for any money whatsoever. I was always independent. I think that has probably always been one of the big motivations for me, that element of showing that I can look after myself.

I never consciously felt jealous of my brother; it was more a question of peer pressure. What I was aware of was being concerned that my father and my mother would expect me to be like my brother. It bothered me a lot, because I already knew that it wasn't for me. I just didn't want to be like my brother. I didn't envy the constant studying and the regimented physical training. It wasn't that I didn't think I could have done it; it was more the routine of it all. For example, I wasn't a bad footballer either and played at a reasonably good standard in the Sunday leagues. Maybe I would have had the talent to go further, maybe not. But it didn't grab me enough – I didn't want to commit to the training side of it. I think subconsciously I probably did take it on board that I wasn't going to be able to compete with Mark, or even want to. It was the same with the academic side. I thought there is no way that I am going to enjoy myself with my nose in a book, when it is something I am not interested in.

I think where I excelled was on the streetwise side of things. I was very independent from an early age. I must have been about ten years old when my mum went back to work as a cook in an old people's home and by then I could sew and wash clothes and I could cook as well. If she wasn't around, it was me who cooked for Dad and my brother and sister. I had watched my mum doing the ironing on a Monday night while we were all watching the football, and I thought that's easy enough. So I would be having a go at a tea towel or a pair of jeans. That way if I needed a pair of jeans ironed, I could do it myself. Even now if I want something done I would rather get it done myself and out of the way. I am not going to wait around. I never thought about whether it was considered a masculine thing to do or not. I just viewed it as necessary, because otherwise I would have to wait until wash day for something I wanted to wear. And far from being called girly, I think by the time you are 14 you get an element of respect if you are going out with your friends to the youth club and you don't have to wait around for your mother to iron your jeans. I was always up and ready and didn't have to hang around and wait. Even at a young age I was also conscious of the fact that Mum had to go to work and then come home and then look after the three of us children. And I think I did make it possible to a certain extent for her to look after Mark with all his studying, and our kid sister Nichola, because I did show her a lot of consideration. Plus, I always got a lot of satisfaction out of being able to look after myself.

Independence was something I valued right from the beginning, especially being able to get out of the house and do my own thing. I had always felt a bit like a caged animal in the house. It was a claustrophobic situation, when all five of us were there. My brother would be upstairs doing his homework and you couldn't run upstairs, shout or play. It would be 'Your brother's working, you've got to do this and that ...' I had to get out, I couldn't stand it. The thought that anybody can put themselves into that much torment just over some bloody exams turned me right off. My brother was up there in his temple of learning, and I just didn't want to be in that environment.

My escape was to go out into the Kent countryside bird watching. Even from the age of five or six I had an instinctive affinity with the countryside. Wildlife programmes were the only things I ever watched, and as I got older the only books I ever read were illustrated bird books. From the age of eight, if I wasn't going to school, I was off out for the day with a couple of mates to go out and find birds' nests. At the time, north Kent wasn't as built up as it is now. I had my favourite areas like Dartford Heath. My parents would say to me, don't go far, but I would be independent and I would always manage to sneak off and find a bus route to take me to the Dickens country round Rochester, out to the salt marshes round there.

My father was always very keen on nature as well. The first place he ever took me bird watching were some beautiful bluebell woods, where the M2 is now. He used to tell me about where he would go to find curlews' eggs and lapwings' nests and watch reed buntings. Now it's all just Thamesmead housing estate, but my dad could remember when it was one of the biggest marshland wader breeding grounds in the country. I loved those stories so much I would get inspired to go further afield – ending up in places I shouldn't have been really at only about nine years old. By the time I started secondary school I was out every weekend. I was gone. I used to take a sleeping bag and stay out overnight. Swanley village was quite accessible from where we lived in Sidcup, and there was still a lot of farmland round there and further out to Fawkham and Brands Hatch. I even went down to Dover occasionally.

So my father realized pretty early on that the worst way he could punish me was by keeping me in the house. I hated that far worse than anything – if I was grounded for two weeks, in 24 hours I'd be like a savage animal. But I always made sure I stayed on the right side of my mum. In the evening, after all we kids had gone to bed, I knew my mum and dad would discuss what had gone on during the day. That was when I hoped Mum would put a good word in for me – and invariably she always did. She always got me out of trouble, but all the way through school, I'm afraid I put her through some pretty sleepless nights. I could not stand Hurstmere School. I fucking hated it, and my behaviour made that pretty obvious. Apart from my first day – when I broke a boy's nose – what used to get me in trouble more than anything was my entrepreneurial activities.

I can't think of a time when I didn't have the instinct to get a little business going. My mum can remember what was probably my first little business, when I can't have been more than eight. We had children's football at the weekend and there used to be a place where you could have tea and little snacks. Well, I got Mum to go down to Macro and buy a load of Kit-Kats and biscuits and I would sell them to the children for a little profit. Then there were the holidays when my dad was doing up some derelict houses and I was helping. I used to check the gas meters before they were broken up, and very often they still had money in them – I must have helped myself to about a hundred and fifty quid in change. So I went out and bought a fishing reel and two pairs of designer jeans – one for me and one for my girlfriend. Even at my first Saturday job I had an enterprise going. I had a job at Fine Fare, which was a supermarket chain in Sidcup. I was the Saturday boy there and I befriended the butcher and we devised a little scam where he would butcher the joints a bit small – never so much as to be noticed – but the extra we'd probably get around five pieces out of each week, which I would then go and sell. So I'd be walking out of the shop with a limp because I had a couple of pounds of fillet steak down my trouser leg.

But there were two incidents really, that ended up sealing my fate at Hurstmere School, and they came very quickly on top of the roofing lead scheme. Oddly enough, the first one was another catering-related earner I had come up with. I had been watching the school canteen, and they had a particular routine. In the morning they would decide what was going to be on the menu for lunch – steak and kidney pies, sausages or whatever – and they would cook them and then put them ready on trays in a hot cabinet. I worked out a way of getting through the fire door, under the preparation table, and opening the hot cabinet. I'd grab two trays of sausages – say there were 75 sausages in each one. That was 150 sausages and I'd sell them in the toilets for 10p each at midmorning break when everyone was hungry. I'd been doing that for about a month and I was making bundles on it.

This was in January, not long after I had gone back to school after running away over the lead scam. I was caught selling the sausages and told to see the headmaster at the end of the day. But during the afternoon, before I had gone up to see him, I threw a snowball up the corridor at one of my friends and unfortunately it happened to hit a teacher, and more or less put him out cold. It wasn't deliberate, because he was actually one of the only teachers I really had a lot of time for. But that really crowned it all. I'd only just got over being absent running away, and then these two events in one day. That was it really for me, and they basically said: 'You're out.' They gave me a letter informing my parents I'd been expelled. So, relying on my mum as usual, I just showed it to her. I don't think she said anything to my dad, but she went into the school the next morning and did a deal with them that I'd be allowed to come back to take my exams that May. I wasn't really worried about the situation. The fail-safe for me in all this was that by this time I had already got a place to learn catering at South East London Technical College, so I only just needed to get basic passes and I was OK, I knew where I was going.

That was quite significant for me, because it was the first time that I actually had a plan. There I was, still at school, but I had the next two years of my life mapped out, already sorted. Though that's probably one of the reasons why I became a full-time proper little bugger for those last months of school! The idea of catering college came more or less from nowhere. It wasn't something I had a burning ambition to do – I had never even really thought about looking at life after school. So when careers came up, I just assumed I would follow my dad into the building industry. I was thinking of being a carpenter or a plasterer because when I had been on building sites, if there was any money it was in plastering.

So I mentioned it to Mum and Dad, and Dad said: 'You'll hate it, I've seen the way you work on a building site and you won't enjoy it.'

Then cooking came up as a simple other option. I'm not sure where the idea came from but I suppose it was because from an early age I'd cooked for myself and the family – and with Mum being a cook, I'd picked up a hell of a lot from her. So I thought, well, why not cooking? I looked at a couple of colleges and applied for South East London Tech, which was in Lewisham, at New Cross in south London. I filled in all the forms, went for the interview which was very simple, and next thing I knew, I was going out to buy all the chef's whites and the gear. So all of a sudden there I was getting on a couple of buses to go to college – bearing in mind that all the time I still had about ten grand from the lead stuffed in a tin under my bed.

I remember going in that first day and it was a revelation. It was all meetings with the lecturers and everything, and everybody was in jeans. This was a breath of fresh air for me. Because it wasn't just at home that I had this caged animal feeling. If anything, it had been worse at school. School had always felt like a prison to me. It was all those rules and regulations. And there was this whole monotonous day-to-day grind where the teachers were fighting such a losing battle trying to teach kids that were like me and my friends. They knew it – and the thing was – we knew it as well. I'm sure there were other ways of going about it, other methods that you could look back at and say, well, perhaps if we'd done this, that guy may have got his O levels. He might have sat down, paid a bit more attention. But the teachers were just there doing 'a job'. It was a boring existence for them too. It's a shame, because you would hope that people are passionate about whatever job they do, especially something like teaching which you can get so much satisfaction from. If I look at the teachers my daughter has now there is no comparison.

For me the two things that summed up the difference between school and college were no school uniform and not being called by your surname. As far as I was concerned that made all the difference – I've never got my head round all that calling you by your surname at school. I could never understand it. Especially at the kind of school I was at, a lot of teachers there would have made a lot more headway with us kids if they'd just used our Christian names. So being called by your Christian name and everything at college, it was all very new. There was a certain amount of theory on the course. We had maths and English, and kitchen hygiene and nutrition, but the rest was really practical. The course I was on was a City and Guilds, which covered everything – including the food service element, which basically meant waitering. You can imagine how well that went down with a bunch of us snotty 16-year-olds – and it was my main downfall, the food service side. I really wasn't interested, and certainly didn't want to be a waiter. I hated that kind of thing.

Along with the lecturing facilities the college had these large theatre kitchens, which were like big hotel kitchens adapted for teaching. And the college had two restaurants, which you cooked in two days a week. In your first year you cooked for the Deptford Restaurant, which was fairly straightforward. Then in your second year it was the Jubilee Restaurant, which was a la carte. The lecturers ate there and so did a lot of local people from the area round the college – the mayor and various businessmen. It was a bargain too, really good food for about £3.50 a head including a glass of wine. I'm not surprised it was a haven for the local businessmen, being able to entertain clients for those sorts of prices. Along with the theory, we used to have practical exams, not just for the cooking side, but unfortunately for food service as well. In my first year I had to do my practical in waiting. It was in the Deptford Restaurant, which had a set menu, and it was nearly all lecturers you served. I had two lecturers examining me and marking me on the way I put the napkin on their lap and everything. So I started serving this guy, he was an Indian gentleman, a lecturer in engineering, I think. But when I started serving him he would kind of nod his head. Everything I did, he'd literally be shaking his head at me. I couldn't handle it and things started to go downhill pretty much from the start, all the way through the whole exam. In the end, I got to the dessert and I put it in front of him and he was doing it again, shaking his head off about the dessert in front of him. So I served the other desserts and I came back to him and I said, 'Have you got a problem?' He said no, but was still shaking his head, which was when I said, 'Why do you keep shaking your head at me?' And that was when the lecturers all got up and asked me to leave immediately, and someone else finished the table. It turned out this poor guy had Parkinson's Disease. That's why the poor bugger was shaking his head.

But I did enjoy the cooking. I can still remember the very first practical cooking lesson. It was from a lecturer called Ian Blake, who must have been in his 30s at the time. He was a very talented chef, and also a really tough-looking bloke, which came as an eye-opener to me after being used to all the teachers at school that you had no respect for. Catering college was a macho place all round. It wasn't sexist exactly – but it was a very masculine environment. All of the male lecturers there had their eyes on the young college girls. The girls would be doing the hotel reception course, waitressing, silver service and stuff like that. And the pretty girls – halfway through the course they knew they were going to be OK, because their good looks would carry them. There were a few guys among the students though, who were good-looking lads and wanted to get to know the girls as much as the lecturers did, so it could all get pretty territorial – a kind of young male lion thing!

Through the first term I didn't have a clue. I just didn't know what I was doing there. I was thinking, what am I doing having lessons in how to cut a carrot? I just couldn't see the point. Even so, the practicals were at least better than the theory classes – hygiene and nutrition, which I hated. I was about three weeks into the course and I had finished my cooking session by about three o'clock one afternoon, and I'd enjoyed it. But we still had two more lectures, one on hygiene and one on nutrition. I was walking down the corridor to get to the lecture room and it was like school all over again and I knew I was going to be bored stiff. I thought, stuff this, I'm going to skive off. So I turned round and that was it. I was basically on my way down the stairs to the foyer to leave when I bumped into the lecturer who was about to take me for the food hygiene class.

He just said casually, 'Hi, Tony. Where are you off to?' It wasn't anything loaded at all. He said it just as you might say, 'Hello, how are you?' He knew full well that I should have been on my way to his lecture, but he still didn't say it like a schoolmaster would say: 'Where do you think you're going?' He was just asking where I was going. So I stopped there on the staircase and my first reaction was the hackles were going to come up and I was going to bluff it out – say something cheeky or pretend I needed to go to the reception desk for something. So I went to say something and it just didn't come out. I was stood there, and I could see the main door and the buses going past outside. I just looked at him and I didn't know what to say. Then he said, 'Look, you know, don't worry about it, you don't have to go,' and I sort of looked at him and said, 'What do you mean I don't have to go?' So he said, 'I know the hygiene's boring, if you don't wanna go, don't go. Just go home. When you do your exams, if you don't know the answers you're not gonna pass the exam are you?' and he just walked off.

That was my first experience of being spoken to like an adult. I stood there watching him walk away, and he didn't look behind him to see if I was following. I could tell exactly what he was thinking: there's another loser who's going to cop out of it. But it was up to me to choose.

Chapter Two

The Heat of the Kitchen

A T THAT moment, standing there on the stairs, with the buses going past outside the entrance, and the lecturer turning and walking up the stairs away from me; that was one of the pivotal moments in my life. It was a turning point really. And I did literally turn round – like something out of a film. I just turned round and walked straight back upstairs, sat down in the lecture, listened to it, took it in, actually understood it. And that was it for me. I thought, this is where it all starts. It was unbelievable, just one of those amazing moments in your life.

That was when it hit me: I'm not in a school environment any more. I've left school. And I still couldn't quite believe it. It's odd. I can remember when I was 26 even, thinking back, 'Christ Almighty, I've left school for ten years'. It takes you that long to shake it off – because I absolutely hated school. And for me, getting that freedom to be an adult was what gave me the chance to blossom. In some ways, I think my dad may have been too strict with me. But he was probably right, because I think he achieved what he wanted to do. If he hadn't put the brakes on when he did, I think I might have been a lot wilder. Instead I was always trying to suss out my dad's next move. Before I got myself into a situation, I would be trying to second guess his reaction, thinking, 'What would my father say about this?' If I knew it was slightly dodgy or I was having a bit of trouble, I'd imagine what my dad's attitude would be. Then I would work my way back from there – from that worst case scenario of being found out – asking myself how bad his reaction would be. That would give me the solution; it was a way of judging the situation.

And now it all came together. I just seemed to be inspired. I got stuck in to starting to get an understanding of the basics of cooking, and I worked really hard. By the time we broke up for Christmas, the penny had dropped. I was actually looking forward to getting back to college after the holidays, and I came back with a completely different attitude. I just couldn't wait to get in the kitchen. I loved watching the produce coming in, I found it genuinely exciting. Sometimes I would end up getting into college early in the morning to see everything arrive – the meat delivery from the butcher's, and the fish and vegetables all coming in. I wanted to know where it was all coming from because I had never been to a market or anything like that. I used to find myself at college at two in the morning watching the vegetables come in. The way it was all boxed up in special crates and everything interested me so much. I just wanted to be around food all the time. And from that time forward I couldn't put a foot wrong.

It was a very classical training, very much the old-fashioned formal way of doing things that you would find in the grand kitchens. One of the things that has made me a lot of money in my career is simplifying those requirements. I have made it easy for a chef just to pick up a piece of pre-cut salmon or meat and cook it without all the disciplines I went through. But at college then in the 1980s, it was still very much the classical cuisine. That meant you were taught right from first principles. So when you were taught to cook a meal you started at the beginning – even if that meant digging up the carrots! It wasn't a question of cooking a piece of steak; you were expected to know how to butcher a whole cow. If you had a recipe for a lamb chop, that meant you had to know all the different cuts of lamb and what part of the sheep they came from. At the time I was also working in a French restaurant in Greenwich, a family-run place, and it was amusing to see all the shortcuts – all the things going on in the kitchen which would have been frowned on at college.

I just worked and worked, and everything started to come together for me. I'd met a girlfriend at college, Mandy, and she used to give me a lift in every morning. We all broke up for the summer and went and got jobs. I was working at Crystal Palace Sports Centre as a chef when the Pope came over, and we were all told to start work at three in the morning. But there was no point in doing any cooking, because none of the Catholics could eat before communion, so I just went out selling drinks which was a good little earner. Then four of us went off on a fishing holiday – Mandy and me, and my mate Rich and his girlfriend – down to Ilfracombe in Devon for a week, fishing and drinking, eating out with the two girls. It was a happy time. We all had a great social life then. I played football for the local pub team and somebody formed a band. When I started working at Crystal Palace we went to a lot of parties, gay parties especially because a lot of the guys around us were gay, and those were some of the best nights out I've ever had. My girlfriend and I would be practically the only straight ones at a party with a couple of hundred people, but they were all great and we had a fantastic time.

The second year was much harder with exams and plenty of theory, but by this time I was spending a lot of time in the kitchen because the college had started to enter me for various culinary competitions all over the place. I was winning quite a few of the competitions, gold medals at the Hotel Olympia show, and so on. There was a big competition for marzipan work which I was pretty well-fancied to win because I was good at all the different marzi-pan fruits. And at the end you had to make and decorate a Battenberg cake, the one where the sponge is quartered in pink and yellow. I was well in the lead, with all the decoration ready and it was just a question of putting the layers together – but I ended up doing pink and pink and yellow and yellow so it looked like halves, not quarters. Of course I got the silver, not the gold, and it took me quite a while to live that down. As well as all the competitions I was the one usually chosen to cook for the special functions for the Mayor, so I had a good reputation. And then in my exams I got four distinctions, which meant I passed out as the top student of my year, 1981.

I think it was a huge relief to my mum and dad. Dad had always had a lot of confidence in me. Right through school he would say to people: that Tony will be the one who cracks it in the end. And Mum had always been very supportive, though deep down she may have had misgivings about what was going to happen next, given some of the things I got up to. She would probably deny it now, but I think it must have been quite a wave of relief for her when I graduated top. My dad was quite mellow, quite relaxed about it, because he'd always expected I would produce the goods in the end. For my parents, with the middle son cracking on, and the older son at university, it was a great moment. But with my brother, things changed. It was as if there had been a subtle shift in the balance of power between us. It wasn't something an outsider would have noticed. Perhaps you might just think, oh, the middle child is the one with the spark. But for the two of us things were different, because it was my turn to be the golden boy. I had been the one who'd had the police all over my ass in my teens. I was the one who'd been a proper little bastard and fucked up school. And all this time he had been the golden child, with his football achievements and his exams and university. Now it was my turn to shine, and he was in the shade, wishing he'd gone professional at football, I think. I'd never really taken on board what a pressure it had been following my brother, but then when for once it was my turn to excel, it was a major thing. Not that I was analyzing it at the time, because the next step for me was truly amazing, which was the plum job in the industry – going to work as a trainee at Claridges. That was how it went from college: the top boy went to Claridges, and the top girl, that was Ruth Harris in my year, went to the Dorchester.

It was the most incredible experience. There I was, this teenage lad from Sidcup, suddenly plunged into working in the kitchen of the top hotel in the poshest part of London. Claridges, at that time, was the jewel in the crown of the Savoy group. It was a private hotel, you had to be invited to come and stay there. And we had proper celebrities at Claridges – I can remember the time when Bing Crosby was actually asked to leave the hotel! Everybody in the industry wanted to work at Claridges. You were right in the heart of Mayfair. Our entrance was at the side, and to get to it you went down this quiet little mews. Then walking into the kitchen was like stepping into another world – this whole village of highly skilled, immaculately dressed, passionate chefs in their tall hats, rushing around, shouting in French.

The head chef then was Felix Subron, a chef of the old school. On my first day he took me into the kitchen and I walked down this corridor, more like a tunnel really, all tiled, and with a ceramic tiled floor. It was like a Tube station – but very, very clean. And the fantastic smell, you could smell the roasted joints. I started at Claridges in September and so they were already well into the game season. It was grouse and partridge and all the rest of the game. And I walked through a plastic curtain and there it was, unbelievable, a new world. Fifty chefs all with immaculate starched white linen aprons and starched white hats. The senior chefs were in their forties or more, and there was a strict pecking order. It was all divided into sections, each with its own head chef and then two sous chefs and then the juniors – five commis chefs.

I was put to work in the larder to begin with, and began work at the bottom, which was second commis chef, earning £57 a week. I had been given a very good piece of advice before I left college – in fact by the same lecturer who had started it all, that day on the staircase, Ian Blake. And he had said, 'Even though you have been working in a restaurant all through college, when you get to Claridges, you know absolutely fuck all, so you keep your head down and do it their way. When you're being shown the way they do stuff, just shut up and listen. And watch what they tell the person next door as well – that way you'll learn twice as fast.'

So I got my head down and cracked on. I kept an open mind. If someone made a fish stock and they might put something in it that wasn't considered to be correct, I just kept my mouth shut. I knew enough not to be giving people an argument at this stage of my career. The sad thing was, though, that when I had been working at Claridges for about three months I got a phone call to say that Ian Blake had died. He'd caught flu, and died from it, and he was only about 40. But in some ways he's the reason I'm where I am now, so I won't forget him.

At about this period I also got a sort of promotion. The sous chef who ran the larder was quite pleased with my work and he started trusting me to do some of the work unsupervised. He would leave the larder to me on Sundays and stuff like that. But Sunday was the busiest day at Claridges. You had the room service, you had the restaurant and there were the residents who lived there permanently in suites. Anyway, there was this Sunday in the summer, where I was running the larder for the day. In the summer we always used to have a cold collation trolley, and it was the same thing year in year out. On the fish side there would be a wild salmon on the Monday. It would be a dressed crayfish on the Tuesday. Then there would be the 'du jour' dishes – all very, very traditional, classical dishes. And on Sunday it was always a cold poached wild sea trout.

This particular Sunday morning the Queen Mother decided to come in for lunch. It wasn't booked or anything, it was just the done thing at Claridges, a lot of famous people and aristocrats would drift in for Sunday lunch. The Queen Mother was quite a regular, and the story was that she always had the wild sea trout. So I heard that the Queen Mother was in and I got the larder perfect – everything was done, all the cold work had been done. It was only about the second time that I had been left in charge on my own. Then what happens but the maitre d' from the restaurant comes down and says, 'Is the trolley ready for when Her Majesty arrives?' This was about quarter to twelve, and service started at twelve with the trolley complete with all the dishes including the two sea trout, poached and dressed and cold. That was when I realized I had been so engrossed in getting the work done I had forgotten to do the sea trout.

So there I am with these two raw sea trout sitting there on the marble. First thing I thought of is, well, I will run over to one of the guys on the saucepans in the starter section and borrow a steamer. But the guy could see I was in the shit, and with the craic like it was at Claridges – it was like a building site – he just looked at me. I can see his face now. He kept a straight face and said, no he's doing the veg. So then I went up to the pastry section said to the pastry cooks, can I borrow a steamer. They were in on to it too, so they gave me the 'Sorry, full up' as well. By this time I'm bang in the shit, this could have been my job as far as I knew. So I thought how the fuck am I gonna get out of this one? I need to get this fish steamed right now. Then I had an idea. I got a high-sided tray and put the sea trout in it, covered with a fish stock bouillon, lots and lots of vinegar and loads of parsley. I sealed it up tightly with cling film. And then I just grabbed it and put it through the dishwasher. Three times through the conveyor belt in that heat, and when they came out they were perfectly cooked. So I got myself out of trouble on that one – I had those sea trout all dressed and ready by quarter past twelve. But I never did find out whether the Queen Mother had sea trout that day.

And of course I eventually got my own back on those guys who'd had the laugh on me. The humour side of it is a big part of working in those famous kitchens. The craic is brilliant. You meet loads of characters and there are pranks going on all the time that could probably lose you your job if you were unlucky. We used to send up the apprentices terribly. For example, the fresh shellfish would come into the kitchen twice a week – crab, lobster and the rest, all alive, and they had to be cooked off. We were having a really busy lunchtime and I saw this apprentice and said to him, 'I'm short of time, would you just run over to the Berkeley and pick up the lobster gun to kill these lobsters for me.' So I've sent this lad all the way to the Berkeley Hotel in Berkeley Square to fetch a lobster gun! It was the equivalent of what would happen on a building site – you'd be sent off to the depot to get a plumber's weight, only to discover it was quite a wait. Another trick I used to do was working in the larder; I would have the apprentice watching, and I would turn the piece of meat round the other way so I couldn't get at it to cut it. Then I'd say, 'I need the left-handed carving knife. It will be in the executive chef's office, you go and ask him for it.' So the apprentice would go off, bang on the chef's door – and the chef would invariably be having a sleep in the afternoon. I know the poor kid's going to get killed. He's going to be absolutely murdered waking the executive chef up to ask for a left-handed carving knife. All that practical joking was fun, but you had to be on your toes. Not only were you expected to produce five star food and five star service in a five star environment, but you had to watch your back all the time. That's what made you so alert. Claridges gave me one hell of a leg up to keep my wits about me; it took me to another level.

Claridges, the kitchen at Claridges, it's a legend – the bastion of everything quintessentially English. And that's not just to a chef that was lucky enough to train there, but to people outside the industry, everybody has heard of Claridges. If you see chefs in a film, working in a grand kitchen, it's always Claridges. And the first time I saw that environment, the atmosphere just hit me. The impact of it was electric – it was like going to a U2 concert. At the time I had this great sense of everybody being totally passionate about food. Of course, if I had been able to stand back and analyze it, probably only about twenty per cent of the chefs loved their work and the rest were just middle-aged bachelors who had been doing it for 25 years, probably drank too much, and were generally in a bit of a sad situation. But of course, it didn't feel like that at the time. There were all these orders being shouted out in French, and you had to remember them, and of course if you were on the veg section, you had all the portions of veg going out which meant you had to know all the French names – epinards, haricots verts, chouxfleurs.

THE HEAT OF THE KITCHEN

To begin with it was pretty stressful until you got yourself into a routine. What I used to do was try to keep pace with all the sections as the orders came in. I used to listen until four or five tables' orders had all come in and keep them all in my head and then start cooking them at once. You could land yourself in the shit if you weren't careful, if you dropped behind with one part of it. But I could get myself so that I was bang on time, and that challenge would make the night go so quickly. You were so into it. What I was doing basically was turning a five hour service shift into three hours of really condensed work. I found I really enjoyed that method, and it worked for me because I could be very quick without losing the attention to detail.

The kitchen was divided into sections, all of which revolved round the hot plate – which is how it is in most kitchens. The hot plate would be where all the dishes came together and then went straight out through the double doors into the restaurant, at which point it is customary to shout 'Ca marche'. That literally means 'It's working' but really it's a signal to the waiter to let him know that the dish is complete and ready to go. The larder, where I began, was right at the back of the kitchen as far away from the stoves as possible to make it easier to keep it cool. The stoves were near the hot plate and they were divided into sections. Roasts was a massive section, and there were also fish, vegetables and sauces. The pastry section was up the stairs, to keep it out of the heat of the kitchen, and round the corner you had the chef's office.

The hours could be pretty long, but it was split into shifts. The easy week was the eight in the morning until four in the after-noon. But after that week you did the 3.30pm until 11.30pm shift, which also included the big weekend nights. When you'd finished cooking in the evenings at 11.30ish you were still buzzing from the adrenalin of this highly pressured environment, so we used to go out all the time after work. We would finish up, jump in the shower and then go off to the nightclubs, which were all thriving at this period in the 80s because everybody, especially the boys in the City, was doing so well. We'd start off at the Bunch of Grapes, which was a fashionable pub in Shepherds Market in Mayfair. Then we used to go on to Browns, or there was an Italian club, the Cinecitta, we liked. Often we would end up at the Covent Garden Piazza and going on to places like The Punch and Judy. Obviously there was no chance of getting home to the suburbs at that time in the morning, so we used to go back to Claridges. A bunch of us who worked the same shifts got friendly with a couple of the night porters and the room service guys, and we squared the duty manager away, so if there was a spare room the six of us were allowed to fall into bed in it. We just piled in completely pissed at three in the morning, and in return we would look after them in terms of food – give them something decent to eat while they were working.

If the hotel was fully booked the other option was the flour sacks at the back. There were two great big bread ovens running through the walls at Claridges. They had been there for about 200 years, ever since the kitchens were built, and that was where the flour sacks were stored. So it was lovely and warm. You'd just find yourself a flour sack, throw a blanket over you and crash out, then wake up in the morning and start work. It was very rough and ready. The thing is that after you've been cooking it can be hard to wind down; you can't just go to bed. You can understand why alcohol and drugs have been rumoured to be rife in the industry. I've got to say to be fair, I never saw one drug at Claridges. But I did see plenty of booze. It was almost encouraged, because we were actually given a beer ration – two bottles of light ale each when you started your shift. But I never used to drink the beer. Instead I used to drink milk all the time. I did that all through my cooking career, milk seemed to give me the energy to keep going.

Life in that big hotel kitchen was non-stop, it was just full blast. And it was brilliant in many respects, even though I only spent eight months at Claridges. One of the most important things was that I met Ronnie Truss, who was later to become my first business partner. He was a very, very talented cook, but he was a maverick and never held down a job for very long. Ronnie worked in some fabulous places though – the Connaught, the Capital Hotel. Pretty soon I was moved out of the larder into the main kitchen to work on vegetables, which meant you could be a lot more involved in everything that was going on. I would be working the veg, but I was already getting interested in fish and I really wanted to get into that section. The chef de partie on fish was a bloke called Mark Jackson, a northerner and a cracking guy. So I started coming in about six hours early to work unofficially on his section before I went onto my section. I wanted to learn everything I could as quickly as I could, because I already knew I wanted to move on from Claridges. Where I wanted to go next was the Dorchester, because at this time, in the early 80s, it was the place to be. Anton Mossiman was the chef there, and he was the new boy in town, with his personal style of nouvelle cuisine hitting the headlines.

So I started to work out how I could get into the Dorchester. I began with the conventional route of phoning the personnel department, but they weren't interested. I needed a name of someone in the kitchen just to get me that little edge. I'd heard a guy called Paul Gaylor was a sous chef there, so I rang the kitchen direct and asked for him. At first he just said to get hold of an application form from personnel, but I said, 'Look, I'm a second commis at Claridges, but I'll come and work for you for free.' So he laughed and said, 'We'd better give you an interview then.' Here I was with a chance to go to the Dorchester, but I was still working on the vegetables at Claridges. I remember saying to the head chef of Claridges, Felix Subron, that I wanted to go and work somewhere that used proper fresh produce. You see in those days, even a top kitchen like Claridges used loads of tinned produce. If you ordered braised celery or braised endive with your restaurant meal, we would go down to the veg store, open a tin, drain it, rinse off the endive or whatever. Then we would dry it with a tea towel and sautee it oil and butter to give it colour. It would go on your plate with butter or sauce and that was it. It was the same with dishes like asparagus soup or braised onions. But that was where chefs like Mossiman were breaking the mould by using real fresh vegetables in their French cuisine. Anyway, Felix said to me, 'I'll show you real French produce,' and this little French geezer marched me down to the veg store and he stood there and said, 'Right, look at all that'.

I looked, and there was row upon row of tinned stuff. You still see it now in French supermarkets, all the Bonneduelle brand. I thought, 'He's done me here'. But in the end Felix Subron really came through for me. Before I could take up my job offer at the Dorchester I needed a reference from Claridges, and that was going to be difficult. Firstly because no Savoy group hotel, including Claridges, would give you a reference unless you had been working for them for at least a year, and I had only done eight months. And even though I hadn't seen much of him, Felix wanted me to stay at Claridges – I think keen chefs were hard to come by. So when I asked him for a reference he just said 'I'll have to think about it'. All the lads in the kitchen were telling me, no way will you get a reference. They'll make you do another a year.

Then one Sunday night we were doing a big party in one of the private rooms and the head chef came in to check everything. We had just started service and I heard this voice over the tannoy, booming out over the kitchen with all the lads listening. It was Felix, the head chef, and he said: 'Allan, your reference is on my desk. Come in here before you leave so you can double check it and make sure I've spelt wanker properly.' That was the last I heard from him, and he'd given me the reference I needed for the next stage in my career.

It was the Dorchester that really got me seriously juiced up about food and cooking. Of course, the routines and disciplines were really no different from Claridges, but the food we were producing was something special. As a kid of only 18 years old it was all tremendously exciting. I think it gave me the realization that you could be innovative with food, which is something that has been an important selling point for me in all my catering enterprises. So the Dorchester was a real take-off, when I knew that the restaurant industry was definitely where I wanted to build a long-term career. Yet I stayed less than a year at the Dorchester. Work in the big hotel kitchens then was a very specific thing, almost like a specialization within the industry, and the working hours and conditions were pretty hard. I had a call from a friend I'd met at Claridges to say he was a sous chef at a City restaurant called Corney and Barrow at Moorgate. The City in the 80s was buzzing, and long boozy, so-called business lunches were the big thing – and the place most people went was Corney and Barrow. Though, admittedly, they went more for the incredible wine list than for the food. Corney and Barrow was the first restaurant venture for Richard Shepherd who had made his name through the wine trade, and it very rapidly became trendy. They had brought in James Rice as head chef who had been at Langan's for five or six years, and he was a great guy.

So I went over there to be chef de partie. Compared with what I was used to at Claridges and the Dorchester it was a very small kitchen, with only five of us in there cooking. The menu was very small too. Thinking back, I suppose the food was pretty mediocre really, but of course the wine list was phenomenal – and that was the whole point! You had guys coming in and spending sixty to seventy pounds a head, which is very difficult to do in a lunchtime restaurant if you are just looking at food. We probably served about 120 people for lunch, with very quiet evenings, but the spend per cover was massive. So the restaurant took seriously good money. For me, having been so centred just on the food side of the business, I think it was a good example of how much more there is to making a restaurant profitable than just cooking well. That's a lesson all chef-restaurateurs have to take on board at some point. I'm not sure whether I consciously realized it at the time, but certainly when it came to opening my first restaurant, Bank, I was very aware of it.

But I didn't learn much on the cooking side at Corney and Barrow. One of the things that had attracted me in the first place was that it was so oriented to business hours, which meant I could get a break from the very long nights I had been doing at the Dorch. And that was how it worked out. I had a really fantastic ten months there, working nine 'til five and I having a hell of a lot of fun. From being quite entrepreneurial at school, I got into the rhythm of picking up a wage packet every week. And it was while I was working at Corney and Barrow that I met my future wife, Denys. By now I felt settled enough that I raided the tin under the bed and pulled out what remained of the lead money. It was enough to put down a deposit on a little terrace house in Bexley, a suburb of south London which still had a very villagey feel. Come Christmas '83 I went into the local, a nice pub called The George in the village of Old Bexley, and there was this girl with the most amazing blue eyes. I was stunned. I saw her eyes right across the bar and I'd never seen eyes like it.

Luckily she was with a guy I used to go to school with, so I was able to go over and say hello. But I was pretty sneaky, as soon as he had gone off to the toilet I started chatting up Denys and there was an instant chemistry there. By the next spring we were going out together. Denys was at St. Martin's College studying fashion and retail with the aim of doing shop window designs. Her style was very individual. At a time when everybody was going round with massive shoulder pads and loads of lycra, she would be in jeans and men's shirts. And I was in jeans as well, and had long hair, which was not a typical 80s look at all. Denys was always very daring in her dress sense, but her figure and her looks meant she could carry it off. And she has a fantastic sense of humour too. We had a great crowd of mates and plenty of time to go out social-izing. It was the same feeling I'd had at college, as if I couldn't put a foot wrong. I had a house, a good career, I was falling in love, eve-rything was in place. And then I had a call from an old Claridges friend, Ronnie Truss.

It turned out that Ronnie was head chef of a new restau-rant being opened by a company called Kennedy Brooks. I think Kennedy Brooks was the first restaurant company to get a stock exchange listing. It was headed up by Roy Ackerman and Michael

Golder. At the time it was very unusual to go public in our industry. I think the Garfunkel's chain was among the first wave to do it, and Bob Peyton's Chicago Pizza group may have been another, but it was quite a new idea. Eventually a lot of the people who were involved in Kennedy Brooks had some very successful spin-offs, like Neville Abrahams and Lawrence Ibbotson who went off to start Chez Gerard. This particular new restaurant, where Ronnie would be head chef, was going to be opened in an excellent location at Bow Lane, on the edge of Covent Garden, and it was called Salter's Court. I went down there to be chef de partie. The restaurant was on two levels with an a la carte downstairs and upstairs a very simple, brasserie-style seafood bar. It was the basic plate of smoked salmon with brown bread or half a dozen oysters. To begin with we had a very good team together. There were four us in the kitchen and an executive chef who used to pop in now and again. But the sort of food that Ronnie wanted to cook was much more modern than the executive chef was interested in and naturally Ronnie was getting frustrated.

I suppose it was inevitable that after a couple of months they had an almighty row and Ronnie ended up being sacked from his position as head chef, which meant I took over as head chef. This was at the time when Kennedy Brooks had just bought the well-known Wheeler's chain of fish and seafood restaurants. With the executive chef quite preoccupied trying to revamp Wheeler's, the management were happy to leave me responsible for the kitchen at Salter's Court, which was fine with me too. But there was one thing that really got to me. Salter's Court was supposed to be predominantly a fish restaurant – and the fish our supplier was sending up to us was terrible. I was a fisherman myself and I used to go casting for sole off the beach on the south coast and did a lot of coarse fishing. I just couldn't believe that we were 50 miles from the sea and people were sending me this shit. I went on and on about it whenever I saw the executive chef. He was an old school guy though, with his preferred supplier, and he just fobbed me off. It was usual throughout the industry for chefs to have their favourite suppliers – not just for fish, but for any of the basics. I don't think there is any line of business that's free of those kind of arrangements.

In the end I just got so fed up with receiving this crap produce that I phoned up a different fishmonger who'd dropped a card in. He was bringing good quality fish up from the coast fresh each week and I bought a load from him. But then the company refused to pay because he wasn't the nominated supplier, and so there was a row going on about who was liable for this delivery of fish. I came in one morning and the executive chef had turned up. I went into his office and he looked up and said, 'Oh, you can go. You've been sacked. I'm sacking you.'

Chapter Three

From P45 to Porsche

I T CAME AS quite a blow. It was 1984 and I was 19. I'd just got my first mortgage and met the girl I was going to want to marry – and now I'd been sacked. But actually that wasn't really what got to me about the situation. OK, I had a mortgage to pay, and at that time I'd been on good money, making about ten grand a year for working nine 'til five. What really annoyed me was basically that they had actually had the audacity to sack me! Me, the golden boy – I mean look where I had worked, all the prizes I'd won and everything. Bolshy little bugger that I was, I thought I knew everything. I considered myself the be-all and end-all in a kitchen. The first thing I did was to book in with a couple of catering agencies to do a bit of temping, which is always available in the industry. And off I went to work a day here and a day there filling in for some junior chef at some pretty basic London restaurant. Oh, those restaurants were awful. After working at Claridges and the Dorchester and top City restaurants like Corney and Barrow, it was just a real downer. But I have never been the type of person to get depressed about things. I think getting angry was a better response than being pessimistic, because it gave me energy, even though the situation was bleak. So I thought, right, I've got a mortgage to pay. How the fuck am I gonna pay it? And that put me right back in the same frame of mind as I had when I was at school, which was to be enterprising.

That was when I sat down and thought about the whole fish thing. After all, I was a promising young chef who'd got himself sacked rather than work with poor quality fish – so there had to be something quite important about supplying decent fish to restaurants. At the time I didn't analyze it very deeply, I just had this instinct that there was money to be made by selling chefs the kind of fish they really wanted. In terms of business theory, of course, what I had done was identify a business opportunity, and now I needed to find a way to develop it. But I never thought of it like that. I never came to it from a theoretical point of view. What I was doing was working very much on a practical level, using personal experience. During my time in the top kitchens I'd been able to observe that even the better end of the London fishmongery scene was not really supplying what the restaurants wanted. None of the fishmongers had much idea of what the end product was – how that wet fish would be prepared to go out to the customer on a plate. So the chefs were always a bit frustrated, and I had a feeling I would be well-positioned to talk to them.

First of all, though, I had to get hold of some fresh fish! I was talking to a friend of mine, Mick Higgins, about it in the pub. He was a carpenter and he had a driving licence, which I didn't at the time. We decided we'd drive down to Hastings, to the fish market, and buy a load of fish straight off the boats. Then we would drive back up to town to sell it direct and really, really fresh. The next market was on the following Monday or Tuesday morning, and that was when we planned to go. The only drawback to the scheme was that we didn't have a van to drive down in, or any money to buy the fish with, even if we got to Hastings. The minimum amount we needed was four hundred quid. Mark reckoned he could get hold of an old van off a mate for about two hundred, and I could get a decent amount of fish with the other two hundred. It doesn't sound a lot of money now, but at the time – even my dad didn't have the cash on him.

I was round at Denys's house, and bear in mind we hadn't been going out long – only a few months. I was telling her about my idea, and I said, 'I'm going to ask your dad if he can lend me the money.' Denys didn't think that was a great idea, but I just ploughed on and said to him: 'Dave, I've gotta buy two hundred quid's worth of fish tomorrow, er, and I need to get a van as well, and we need to pay for the van too, so could you see your way to, er, can I borrow – four hundred quid?' It was cheek, but luckily for me Denys's dad, David Gainsford, just thought it was funny, and he went upstairs and came back down with £400. So Mark and I were in business. We'd got the van, an old red Morris 1000, and I had me two hundred quid for the fish.

Three o'clock the following morning, we were up and on the A21 down to Hastings. But the whole thing was nearly a disaster before we even started. We got caught in traffic and by the time we reached the coast we were running late. Obviously I didn't want to miss the auction, so I just got Mark to drop me off at the dockside for the market and I went in while he went to park the van. With a fish auction, the seafood is all there in trays, straight off the boat, and what you have to remember is that it is 'Dutch auction'. That is, the price starts high and the auctioneer gradually reduces it until someone makes a bid. It's all quite confusing at first. The fish is sold in kilos, which I'd hardly heard of. And a lot of it goes to France and Spain, so there are always a lot of heavy-duty export guys there. The auctioneer might start at something like £16 a kilo – a ridiculous price – and then it would get down to about £6 a kilo. That's when you'd shout and you'd buy two four-stone boxes of sole, or whatever they're auctioning. It is all a case of nerve. People with big export orders to fill or a high profile client in London would be inclined to jump in early because they didn't want to miss out and risk not filling their order, and that could push the price up.

That first morning it was a bit intimidating. I was standing there, this unknown newcomer in my jeans and sweater, surrounded by all these weathered fishermen in their pea coats. But I'd managed to work my way into the line in front of the boxes of fish where the auctioneer was standing. Then I saw Mark come in at the entrance, so I waved at him to show him where to come, and that was it – the auctioneer's gone: BANG, Sold. So we were in trouble. First off, I didn't have anything like the money to pay, and secondly I'd paid three times the going rate. So that was my first experience of buying fish at auction. Luckily Mark just went straight round to the auctioneer and explained what had happened. I think partly because we were so young, the auctioneer said he'd let us off just the once. I ended up buying £200 worth of Dover sole that day. Half of that we'd sold out of the back of the van before we even got back into town, and the rest we sold to a London restaurant. We ended up with £500 in cash by lunchtime. Working as a chef I think the maximum I'd ever earned in a week was £200. So there it was, suddenly I had just turned over my weekly wage in a single day. David Gainsford got his £400 loan back in two days.

We started going down to Hastings on a regular basis, three times a week. We would buy Dover sole or whatever fish the boats had brought in. Hastings was known then for its flatfish – sole and plaice – but when the cold weather came around, it was cod. Then we'd run it straight up to London to sell direct and make a profit, just the two of us and our old van. That first time going down to Hastings had shown us it would work. I had confidence in the idea right from the start. I knew that, as a chef myself, I was in the right position to be able to talk directly to restaurant chefs and have a meaningful conversation about what they needed, which they hadn't been getting from the traditional fishmongers. If you were describing this as a business model, its great virtue is that it was a very straightforward and simple proposition. I spotted a gap in the market. Then I got an interest free micro-loan of £400. Of that, I made a capital investment of £200 – the van. The other £200 was spent on acquiring stock – the fish – and on that expenditure I made more than one hundred per cent profit. And the unique selling proposition that drove my success was a thorough knowledge of my chosen business environment. Or you could say that I was a desperate young chef with a mortgage and a girlfriend, who bought a load of fish and sold it to his mates.

Whichever way you look at it, the end result is: we had a business. But it was only around four weeks before the honeymoon period was over at Hastings. They'd tolerated us when we were a bit of a joke – two young lads who didn't know anything. But pretty soon they turned round and said: you're not welcome anymore, simple as that. And you don't argue with those boys. Luckily though, I had built up a bit of a relationship with one guy who was buying down there and he said he'd buy for us. By this time we were already beginning to build up a steady clientele. It was nothing dramatic, just a few little London restaurants, nothing well known. But they were saying: can you get other stuff? We were doing the well-known fish like cod and plaice in quite large quantities, but they also wanted some of the more fashionable fish – red mullet, salmon and so on. If we could supply them with all the different varieties they needed for their menus and still maintain the freshness and the good price we were offering with the fish from Hastings, we knew we had a good chance of becoming the regular fishmongers for these restaurants.

So this was when we started to go to Billingsgate, the big London fish market, which was a major step. Everything was happening so quickly and we had to react really fast to keep up with ourselves. Because the other problem we had was that we didn't have any kind of base – we were still working out of the back of the old van, which was literally all we had. We needed somewhere to do all the knife work that's associated with fish preparation: gutting, scaling, filleting and eventually cutting up into steaks and portion sizes. Just round the corner from where I had bought my house was a council estate called St Paul's Cray, which had a pretty dodgy reputation. I didn't care about that though, because it had exactly what we needed: an old fishmonger's shop which had been closed down for about six years. We spoke to the council and they said to us that we could have a rent free period in which to do it up. They would then send a health and hygiene inspector round, and if we passed the check, we could rent it – I think it was about two and a half thousand a year, so fifty quid a week.

We struck lucky straight away because St Paul's Cray was one of those south London estates which had been created for East Enders after the Blitz, and over the 30 years or so they hadn't lost their taste for fish and seafood. The jellied eels, the piece of fish on a Friday and shellfish were old Cockney traditions and people hadn't forgotten them. So when we opened a retail outlet at the front of this place – it was in Coppendene Crescent – everybody came. On a good week we were taking about a thousand pounds at the front, while at the back we were preparing the wet fish to go up into town for the restaurants. Quite early on we got big orders from Corney and Barrow and another restaurant called The City Circle.

From that first day down at Hastings, with nothing but an old red van and two hundred quid in cash, almost overnight we had got to the position where we had premises, and about 15 regular customers. I had even had to get a little answer phone so people could phone up and leave the next day's order while we were down the market buying or in the back doing preparation. Very rapidly it got to the point where some days we were selling five to six thousand pounds' worth of fish wholesale and taking four to five hundred quid at the shop in the front. I was drawing enough money out of the business to pay my mortgage, plus 40 quid living expenses each week, and ploughing everything else back into the business. At this stage I really didn't have the expertise in the business management side of it at all, I was so inexperienced. I was giving a week's credit and sometimes even a month or more. Trying to get clients on board I ended up giving too much credit, which put us in a sticky situation, even though business was so good.

We had to borrow money from Mick's dad in the end, and we owed him about £5,000. For a small business, like ours, just starting up, it is easy to get carried away with all the new clients coming in – but the credit management is vital right from the start, something a business school would tell you straight away, but obviously something I had no knowledge of. At one stage we must have owed Billingsgate about £17,000 – but at the same time we had clients owing us around £25,000. I worked out that if I paid the market and repaid Mick's dad his loan, I would only end up with a couple of grand to show for this really good business I'd started. I think you could identify that as one of those crucial periods that any small business goes through, where the numbers just don't really add up, but to an extent you just have to go with your guts. This was the point where Mick was finding it all a bit too much. He was a carpenter by trade after all, and the whole culinary aspect of it was a closed book to him. And that's when Mick just said to me one day, 'Look, I'm gonna go, you know I want to get back into the building game.' So I paid his dad back and started thinking about what to do next.

Ronnie Truss had always been one of my best mates, way back from the Claridges days, so I phoned him and said, 'What are you doing?' It turned out that he'd had enough of the big restaurant kitchens and he'd opened his own snack bar in Petticoat Lane, which wasn't going as well as he'd have liked. So we got together and I told him what I was up to and that I needed a partner, and he said 'All right, let's go for it then.' Ronnie got twenty per cent of the company, escalating to thirty per cent in a few years' time, and his job was what the experts would call 'marketing'. To us that meant Ron going out and about all day in the van, not just doing deliveries, but elbowing his way into kitchens to make cold calls on the chefs. We had to expand or the whole thing would have died on its feet. So we started by approaching a lot of old friends from Claridges and the Dorchester. By that time a lot of them had moved off to take promotions in smaller restaurants, which worked out well for us because it meant they were in the position to give us orders, which they could never have done if they had still been with the big boys. We didn't carry any clout in the industry at all at this stage – we were just two young enthusiastic ex-cooks, a bit disillusioned with kitchens, and with an interesting idea. We always believed there was a massive gap in the market, because the fishmongers that were supplying into London restaurants were still very stuck in the mud. But you could see that within the next couple of years there was going to be a massive culinary explosion.

This was the mid-80s and you could just feel the atmosphere, there was change everywhere. Chefs had gone from being this archetypal pot-bellied guy with the big white hat to young kids in their 20s in jeans. Gary Rhodes was just starting to make a name for himself at The Castle in Taunton, and all the old stuffiness was going out the window. And there was David Cavalier, and then Marco Pierre White. It was a really sudden change in the industry that took hold in 1985/86, just at the time that we were getting going. The first top restaurant we got as a client was Walton's, in Walton Street, which had a Michelin star, and that helped build our reputation a lot. But in itself this had a knock-on effect, as most of the restaurants we were supplying were in London, and especially in the City. Which meant driving up from Sidcup to Billingsgate to buy the fish, then going all the way back through the Blackwall Tunnel again down to St Paul's Cray to do the preparation, then turning round and taking it back up to town again. It became obvious that we were going to have to move out of Coppendene Crescent – even though it had been good to us – and get ourselves somewhere in central London. In 1986 we managed to find an old meat warehouse on the edge of Smithfield market – about the only one of the traditional fresh produce markets which hadn't moved out of London proper. It was just a concrete building with a drainage channel on the floor, and it was about to be demolished, but we got it under a monthly licence.

It was only just over a year since I had been sacked, but by 1986 it was all happening. The business had made it into London and we had given it a name: Cutty's. My brother had just left university, and I was able to offer him a job doing the books – I was determined not to let the accounting get out of hand the way it had before. And to crown it all, Denys and I got married that

August. We didn't even have a honeymoon. I remember getting married, coming back in on the Saturday night after the wedding, taking down all the orders off the answer phone, then getting going on Monday's orders. This was the same time that Ronnie made a massive breakthrough for us by getting the order from the Barracuda Club Casino. That was the explosion for us, when business went absolutely mad. After the Barracuda, we got the London Park Tower Casino, because they were both in the same group. Then we went on to get the other big one, which was The Victoria Sporting Club.

For us they were highly profitable orders because the thing about casinos at that time was 98 per cent of the food and drink was complimentary to people who were gambling. So someone would get on to the roulette table and of course they'd order two grilled Scotch lobsters – it was what you did. So the casinos would need 30 or 40 lobsters a day and in the winter they could be really hard to find. But we had all our contacts down in Hastings and so we made damned sure we got them. That's how our reputation began to build as these two guys who could get you anything, even if it might be at a price. By the end of the year though, the Smithfield premises were due to be demolished, so we had to move practically overnight.

Our 'offices' still consisted of the answer phone back at my house in Sidcup, so that wasn't a problem, but it was going to be difficult to find somewhere we could afford that would have enough space for the amount of food preparation we were doing. And that was when we found 683 Old Kent Road, an old jellied eel shop. It had a big walk-in cold room, which was just what we needed. We quickly put a fish cutting block in there and some hoses – and that's when we really went to work. We'd got it all in place. We had the casinos' orders; we had our regulars among the restaurants. I think that first year of Cutty's at Old Kent Road we must have turned over £300,000. By the second year it was up to £750,000 – but even that was really only the start of things. Ronnie and I were sitting down in the back at 683 Old Kent Road, having a chat. He said to me, 'Look, let's really go for it. Let's get the business of every Michelin star restaurant and every five star hotel.' Well, then after that it just went ballistic.

We had all our regular customers, and we had our one Michelin customer, which was Walton's, and then we just went for it. We went for Marco Pierre White, we got his order. Then we got Michelle Roux at the Waterside Inn at Bray; then Raymond Blanc, and Pierre Kauffman and Christian Delteil and Nico Ladenis. We went on this sort of culinary quest to get every accoladed restaurant we could, and then from there we went on to Park Lane, the five star hotels. It helped a lot that we both had good friends and contacts within the industry. Take Mark Hix, who is now famous as one of the owners and executive chef of Le Caprice. Mark was one of my early customers. It was when I was working in the shop in St Paul's Cray, Ronnie hadn't even come on board at that time. I'd heard about this restaurant in the City where they used fresh foie gras, and in those days you just never saw that at all. Even at Claridges the foie gras would have been in a tin. To do a tournedos Rossini, you'd cut a slice off and stick it on the top and that was it. So I phoned this guy Mark Hix, and he said, 'Yeah come along and have a chat.' We got on so well we ended up going for a beer together and became good friends. Mark turned out to be one of the most level-headed and successful chefs of the time. He was one of the most influential cooks in my career; certainly the first that

I thought was absolutely brilliant. He was so innovative; his cooking was years ahead of his time.

He was also one of the first people that I cold-called. Right from the beginning of my career, when I rang the Dorchester, I have always believed in cold-calling, and certainly, with Cutty's, there was often no other way of getting orders. I remember one day Ronnie said: 'Why don't we just go through the Yellow Pages?' So we were looking at the gentlemen's clubs, all the Pall Mall addresses like the RAC Club and The Athenaeum, all that. You would ask to be put through to the chef, and you'd get knocked back straight away. It was just becoming a joke in the end. We were on our tenth or twelfth club, and we'd got the beer out by then, and Ronnie found this one, The Strategic Planning Society, with a Pall Mall address. So he rings it, and they pick up the phone, and he just said straight off: 'Can you tell me what your next move is please?' and of course, we just collapsed. That was one of Ron's strong points. He had a brilliant, fantastical sense of humour. And a lot of times, it was only humour that got you through. There would be days when you were beginning to feel really down – you couldn't get your money in, and Billingsgate needed paying – but Ron would always find the funny side.

It may not have worked with the gentlemen's clubs, but cold-calling got us through the kitchen door of a lot of the top restaurants, mainly because we wouldn't take no for answer. We'd drive them mad, until they would see us just to get rid of us. We had a lot of cheek too. We'd got a catering order for the Silverstone grand prix course which was ultimately worth a hundred grand to us, and we went up there to make the first delivery, and then back again later to collect the boxes and tidy up. We were driving back and we realized how close we were to Raymond Blanc's Le Manoir

Aux Quat' Saisons, just outside Oxford, which is one of the best of the best restaurants in Britain. At the time Raymond was pioneering nouvelle cuisine and was very talked about. So Ron said, 'Oh let's drop in for dinner at Le Manoir', and that's what we did – both of us in jeans, stinking of fish. And we were terrors; we demanded to go into the kitchen and chat to the chef, and sure enough, we started supplying them. Only little bits and pieces at first, but eventually Raymond Blanc became one of our regular clients.

Apart from cold calling, there was another technique I started using once we could afford it. I used to corner the market in various fish. I would get into the market an hour before they'd even started and go round and buy, say, every bit of large bass there was, or every scallop in the shell. I wasn't even bothered if I paid a bit over the odds, because I knew that later on in the day the chefs would be looking to their regular fishmongers for bass or scallops and they wouldn't be able to get them. That's when we would get the call, and a chance to start supplying regularly – because the first couple of times you would supply them 'as a favour' and then after that you would insist on being made their regular supplier. You get this kind of cartel trading in different markets all over the world – but at the time I never thought of it as one of those recognized business procedures that I could use. I just did what seemed the obvious thing. And fish is a very natural market to work, because unlike most of our food, fish is hunted much more than it is farmed – and that means that there can be shortages. If the men on the trawlers have had a bad trip, then the fish just isn't there in the market. So for a fishmonger to be able to guarantee to fill his orders was worth a lot to the customers, and at Cutty's we prided ourselves on very rarely writing 'Not Available' on our delivery notes.

It wasn't just buying stuff up; I used to do everything I could think of to make sure we had the produce when nobody else did. I used to watch the long range weather forecast and that would give you an idea of what the catch was likely to be out at sea. And then there was the whole art of predicting demand. We used to have a lot of people tipping us off about what was going to be on menus. Ronnie used to talk to chefs weeks in advance, especially in the big hotels where functions were booked and planned many weeks ahead. Ronnie would be over at the Hilton on Park Lane, chatting with a chef, 'So what have you got coming up? I expect December is going to be busy again.' If the Hilton is having a big banquet, and you have around a thousand people who are going to be sitting down having turbot, that's a lot of fish. Particularly with fish like turbot that are hard to portion up economically. So if we got the tip off about it, we would be all around the coast – down to the West Country, or all the way up to Aberdeen – buying up turbot ready for when the order went into the market. Then it would go round all the suppliers that there was a buyer in London that wanted a lot of turbot in the next couple of weeks and the price would go mad.

You had to be careful how you bought, so that people didn't realize what you were doing. What helped us there was our knowledge of fish. People imagine fish has to be eaten immediately, but for wholesalers like ourselves, buying it straight from the sea, we could store it carefully and keep it at the peak of freshness for as long as two weeks. This was really what got us into those big, five star hotels with their massive functions. We were starting to buy direct from Cornwall. It was risky though, because at this time, towards the end of the 80s, there was an unwritten law at Billingsgate that if you bought direct from the coast you weren't welcome at Billingsgate. If we'd still been the small outfit we were when we started, it could have been a real problem. But luckily we were now so big, and owed Billingsgate so much money, that we had got ourselves into a position where challenging us would have damaged them more than us.

I remember when I realized for the first time exactly what a big opportunity the hotel market offered. It must have been around 1989 and I was trying to get the account at the Meridian Piccadilly. They finally phoned for some large sea bass, which their regular supplier couldn't get. Luckily I did have some truly amazing, unbelievably fresh bass just in, so I rushed it round. I'd hardly got back to Old Kent Road when the phone went. It was the Meridian: 'Come and collect this fish. We can't use this, it's frozen.' Of course it wasn't frozen, it was just so fresh it still had rigor mortis – but they didn't have a single chef in the kitchen well enough trained to spot it. And that told me the market was ours for the taking, if we did it properly. I realized that the hotels had different requirements from the Michelin starred restaurants. We had a couple of three star restaurants and quite a few, maybe around 50, with one or two stars, and they weren't big orders. So if I had bought, say, a few tonnes of turbot from down the coast, or several tonnes of sole, you'd always pick out six that were beautiful, absolutely perfect and still stiff, and they would go off to the restaurants. You didn't need a rock solid stiff, rigor mortis turbot or sea bass to supply a five star hotel, so the hotels would get the rest of the batch – still the highest quality, very fresh, but more relaxed. In fact, those fish often eat better anyway. So everybody was happy and we gained a reputation for dealing only in the very highest quality fish, for which people were prepared to pay a premium.

But 683 Old Kent Road wasn't really looking the part, it needed doing up a bit. We were turning over so much business at the time that we really had to watch the catch flow, so we decided to get a bank loan for the decorating. I went down to my NatWest in Sidcup to see the bank manager. He was quite a small guy, like a jockey almost, and all I can remember was looking at this vast expanse of white collar and a tightly-knotted tie, with a little head and neck perched on top – a bit like a ventriloquist's dummy. He's sitting there with this fixed smile looking at these two long-haired guys in shorts and t-shirts, stinking of fish (as usual). And we said, 'Um, we want to do our place up in the Old Kent Road.' He asked, 'Well, how much do you want?' I said – I don't know why, because we were only thinking of a couple of coats of paint – 'Fifty grand, but we'll put in twenty'. He just said, 'All right, the bank will lend you forty'. So there we were with the money burning a hole in our account and I remember saying to Ron, 'Let's get someone in to tosh the place out cheap and we'll get a car.' And we went and bought a Porsche each with the loan. We matched the bank's £40,000 with £10,000 of our own and bought two three-year-old Porsches for £50,000. That was what you might call our first major move in the world of financing!

It was symbolic though, of how far we'd come. To analyze it in business terms, what I had done was spot a gap in the market and a particular skill set I could bring to it. I got the micro-loan I needed to get started, and I had it all before me – I was determined I was going to get somewhere. Looking back, so much happened in the space of just twelve years, but you never think about it like that at the time. Ronnie and I were basically two very hungry young men on a mission to supply all the country's top restaurants. Yet we instinctively did things right, from a business perspective. We didn't over-capitalize early on. We never spent a lot of money on premises. If anything they were always lagging behind the quality of the product. And we didn't go mad taking on a lot of staff early on, so were always keeping our overheads and costs down as far as possible. We kept on putting as much as possible into the product itself. We knew perfectly well that was what we were all about – the best fish, to the best places. That USP had developed so quickly and become so well known, that it was always going to be a priority. We were guys who knew about fish, and we knew enough not to mess with that.

The kind of Hollywood side of it – the two long-haired young guys delivering fish in open-top Porsches – wasn't deliberate, but it was probably inevitable, because that was the way we were. If you needed fish for your restaurant at nine o'clock at night, one of us would turn up at the kitchen door in the Porsche, but always with the fish you wanted, when you wanted it. If Nico had run out of something at Chez Nico or Michelle needed more lobsters down at Bray at the Waterside Inn, then Ronnie would be there with it. We made sure we always delivered, 24/7. Without even realizing we were doing it, the whole Porsche thing became a bit of a marketing gimmick. We suddenly found we had this reputation around the West End. Hotel managers and restaurant owners would say, 'Oh, you mean the two young fellers that deliver fish in a Porsche.' Some people were probably thinking, if they can afford to deliver fish in a Porsche they're obviously charging us too much money. But the majority of our clients thought it was fabulous, they just enjoyed the theatre of it – turbo-charged scallop delivery by sports roadster! To us, it was just our working day; since we'd been mad enough to go and buy these cars we had to use them. It wasn't until a big fishmongers company came all the way from

Australia to see how we worked that we realized what we'd started. They were called the Flying Squid Brothers, and they came over to London to look at the restaurant scene and meet these two guys who'd taken the West End restaurant scene by storm. That was the first we knew that we were being talked about so much.

By the time we reached the end of the 80s we were well on course. We had a blue chip list of customers by now, but there was still more work to do. There were a couple more five star hotels we wanted, and we were still on our quest to get all the Michelin starred restaurants. And then the recession began to hit. I immediately thought: this is going to hit us. The first thing that's going to happen is that our niche market will go tits up, because the boys won't be out to lunch in the City spending £75 a head. And the girls aren't going to be over in Kensington having £50 lunches. So we cut back on all our overheads and we kept everything very, very tight for a year. I think we had the same turnover in '88 as we did in '89, and we just went with it. One of the things that helped us to ride it out was that we had quite a broad base of customers. In some cases the size of the orders went down. You could see that some of the receipts coming in from the fine dining restaurants were smaller. Famous chefs with trendy little places down in Battersea were no longer attracting people out to spend £70 or £80 a head for a meal. Top guys like Danny Cavalier and Christian Delteil were batting on a sticky wicket. Marco was suffering in Wandsworth. All of them, they didn't have it as good as in the mid-80s.

The restaurant business had to change a lot to cope with the recession. The core produce the chefs were using had to change, as did the style of restaurant. Instead of putting a few bums on seats and serving up pricey ingredients like foie gras and scallops, the restaurants needed to do more covers each night and find ways of selling diners on cheaper ingredients like offal and vegetables. In order to adapt to the change in the market, we needed to diversify. As we started to come out of the recession around 1990 I took on a guy called William Black. To protect the business I needed to increase turnover, and that meant finding new angles on what we supplied, and broadening the customer base. William was married to the chef and restaurant writer Sophie Grigson, and they'd already done a couple of TV series together.

I had seen a documentary about William going over to France to buy specialist French brasserie ingredients direct from the producers. He had this flat in Maida Vale and he would go over to France in a big three-tonne van and just fill it full of produce – everything from milk-fed pigeons to live zander, and rillettes and boudins blancs. At the time we still had this wish-list of about 25 customers that we just couldn't crack. It was very trendy restaurants like Kensington Place and in-chefs, including Alistair Little, and these guys basically didn't want to know about us. They liked dealing with people from their own background that they had always known – and that basically meant William, because they had all gone to university together. So they liked going down and buying their stuff from some little place in Rye, where you had to be in the know, and they liked William Black. It was very much a case of building the menu around what interesting stuff he had available. He used to get hold of the most brilliant produce, but William was a terrible businessman.

So we suggested to him to come and work for us, and I think William thought it would be an easier life, so he did. I remember we paid him what felt like a massive salary at the time, which was about forty grand a year. But it was worth it to us because he could get us stuff like blue fin tuna that we could sell to the Japanese restaurants. It worked – within a couple of months our turnover had gone up by about £15,000 a week. Plus we had William's client list, and a whole new range of suppliers out of France. Now we really were the only show in town. I suppose effectively what we had done was expand by buying out a smaller rival, which is something you see done in the High Street every day. But to me it was just sheer culinary egotism. I just said to myself: 'I want William Black's customer list. I want the produce that William Black's got.'

That was basically how Ronnie and I ran the business at that stage. We didn't have any theory or business training behind us, but we just knew what we could do, and our skills complemented each other. Ronnie was customer liaison and marketing. You can call it what you want, but the fact was that Ronnie was a brilliant salesman. And he was helped a lot by the fact that our product was so good that it more or less sold itself – if you could get your foot through the door. And the product was my department – I had a natural talent for buying the right stuff. I was probably the best around at that time. Our other big plus was that we both had a lot of all-round expertise in the restaurant industry. Ronnie had great social skills at communicating with the chefs, and he also had comprehensive culinary knowledge to go with it. To this day I've never met anybody with such a brilliant set of taste buds as Ronnie – and he's a fabulous cook. His methods left a lot to be desired, as did the trail of mess he used to leave, but he's a great cook all the same. I think what I brought to the party was that I was very sharp, and very switched on – and totally driven. Over this whole time, from when I was sacked back in 1984, to the early 90s when Cutty's became dominant in the market, a period of about ten years, I didn't have a holiday. I'd grab the odd Bank Holiday with Denys and the kids. The rest of the time my day began with crawling out of bed at two-thirty in the morning. I would get back home at about three o'clock in the afternoon and sleep until six in the evening. Then it was the kids' bedtime, so I would spend an hour with them, and then straight off out again. Usually it would be to go to a client's restaurant for dinner to network. Looking back Denys and I probably ate out every night on the trot for five years.

By the time the industry came out of recession in the early 90s, the world had changed. Restaurateurs had to be better businessmen as well as chefs. They had learnt how to reduce their overheads so that they could increase the profitability on turnover. Now it was Terence Conran who was leading the way with big brasserie-style restaurants with many more tables and using simpler, cheaper ingredients in the menus. He opened Mezzo in about 1994, and it was one of the biggest restaurants in Europe. It was a real ground-breaker, with a fantastic head chef, John Tiraud, who went on to have a television career and open a very successful restaurant, Smith's, at Smithfield Market. This meant that as suppliers, our job became different too. I remember John asking if he could send some guys down for training. What had happened was that this new style of very busy, pared-down kitchen couldn't waste time training up apprentices in things like how to fillet different varieties of fish. At the same time the City & Guilds training that I had gone through had stopped. So, not only were the new massive restaurants not getting fully-trained chefs, but they certainly didn't have the time to train them up on the job. And that was when we realized that we had a new market, not as fish suppliers, but as a training college for fish chefs. This became another diversification for us, using our skilled fish chefs at Cutty's in the Old Kent Road to train chefs for our clients' restaurants.

By now though, we had a real problem with our Old Kent Road premises. For anybody who came into London from the south, Cutty's was becoming famous for the wrong reasons. Ask any cabby and he'll remember the time when you would be coming in on the Old Kent Road and get as far as Cutty's at about three o'clock in the morning and the whole road would be full of fish! There were articulated lorries, our two Porsches parked on the pavement, and just pallet-loads of fish all crated up. By eleven o'clock that morning it would all be gone – either in the fridges or sold already. That was the way we were working and we were doing such a hell of a volume. Worse than that was the whole hygiene issue. We'd grown so quickly and got all these five star hotels on board, but that meant we were beginning to fall foul of the regulations. The European Union kept on coming out with one directive after another on food hygiene, preparation and handling, and it meant that the Hilton and the rest couldn't legally go on buying from us. You'd get calls from the executives at the Lanesborough and the Savoy saying, 'Listen, lads, when are you going to move? We're pushing it as it is. You've got to do something.' We were breaking the law, basically, and it got to the point where if we didn't do something – and quickly – we were going to get done.

Chapter Four

Banks, Bankers, and Bank Restaurant

INTEREST RATES were pretty high in the early 90s so we kept putting the move off and putting it off, even though we knew we had to bite the bullet at some point. The help we got from the customers was unbelievable. There were five star hotels that shouldn't really have been continuing to buy from us while we were working out of the Old Kent Road, but we promised we would be moving, and they held on. Some of them were even offering us money to get a new unit, which at the time I naively thought was very kind of them. In retrospect I can see that they would have loved to buy into our business. We kept on looking for a place, but with 15 per cent interest rates, it was really hard finding somewhere. Finally, in 1992, we found a unit round the back of Old Kent Road. Thanks to the hygiene rules we would more or less have to build the equivalent of an operating theatre from scratch, but we thought we could do it. I used to get so frustrated that any guy in a street market could still have a barrow and cut up a bit of fish in a bucket of water, but we were breaking the law – as if the guy on the street is going to be more hygienic just because he does a smaller turnover.

In the end of course, the regulations forced us into building something that was totally amazing – a state of the art fish supply premises. It was really something new because we designed and built it along the lines of the great kitchens, just like Claridges, where Ronnie and I had first met. It was the only system we knew. We weren't logistics experts, but it worked brilliantly. We had a central glassed-off area where my brother, Mark, would sit with a microphone. From two o'clock in the morning he would be calling out the orders: 'Le Caprice, two dozen bream; The Savoy, 30 lobster,' just as if he was a sous chef calling the table orders to a kitchen. Our equivalent of the chefs all had their sections – but instead of roasts or whatever in a restaurant, it was the fridges with the different varieties of fish and seafood. They would bring the produce out and assemble it into the correct orders on racks (our version of the traditional kitchen hotplate) and then it was loaded into the vans for delivery. There were 12 van loads of fish at a time going into the London restaurants. Meanwhile, I would have gone to the market and come back with a hell of a lot of fish. I would be arriving with two van loads of fish to be prepared and got ready to sit in the fridges – which was like the larder work I'd done way back at Claridges. So it was exactly the same system as a five star hotel. When it was all ready we invited all the major chefs in London to a grand opening party. All the produce was on display. I remember we had the Cutty's logo done in tiles on the floor and it looked great – it was a proud moment.

At the same time though, I was under huge pressure. Billingsgate was a cut-throat place. When you are buying a quarter of a million pounds worth of fish every week you can't afford to relax for a second. If you had an extra glass of wine at dinner, that could easily put you a beat behind at three o'clock the following morning when you were bidding for fish. And I was doing everything – the pricing, the margins – in my head the whole time. I never even used a calculator until about 2000, but I could work out the bottom line to within half a per cent of what the accountant would come up with on the computer. So you had to stay completely and utterly on the ball, regardless of sleep or anything. People would say, 'I suppose you get used to having to get up at that time.' Believe me, you never do, especially not with a wife and two young children, all trying to lead a normal life. Right from the beginning, it was like being thrown into a shoal of great white sharks. And now Cutty's was doing so well, those sharks began to circle.

The first thing that happened was we heard that there was someone in Billingsgate who wanted to buy us. We didn't have a clue about what to do in that situation. Should we sell? Should we part with a percentage? How much should we ask? So the bank manager recommended a financial consultant, and this turned out to be Jeremy Omerod. Jeremy came in and checked us out, and the first thing he said was, 'You'd be mad to sell this business, it's a gold mine.' So he ended up coming on board as our financial advisor and he showed us how to use debt properly and how to distribute our money. Really he took us from being just this cash-creating outfit going at a hundred miles an hour, to becoming a properly established business.

Cutty's was flying, but we couldn't afford to sit still. We had to keep developing and expanding. Already I'd started to see some competition come into our market. Like any business, we knew that there would be other suppliers looking to copy what we were doing and that they would soon be coming up behind us. I felt we had only a matter of two or three good years left – perhaps four at the most – before we would have to do something else just to maintain our position. In fact it wasn't even a matter of maintaining that position, because I don't think we could have just gone for maintenance. In our business there were six or seven reputable London companies, family businesses, that had kept about the same turnover for the last five or six years. They were finally getting wise to the new marketplace and were beginning to creep up on us. We started seeing a big order shared here, and somewhere else we would have to fight a tender process. We had to start quoting prices, and those prices had to be competitive. In business terms, it was one of those crucial times where consolidation is not an option – you either grow or you will gradually lose your market position.

I didn't need anyone to point that out to me. It had always been the same with Cutty's. Every time there was a turning point I had known I had to come up with something new, even if it meant taking risks. At this point we were totally committed to the whole-sale trade – the restaurants and the hotels – but I hadn't forgotten the success of that little fish shop in St Paul's Cray, back when we were just starting out. So I wanted to get a more direct link into the consumer, to be able to do retail as well as wholesale, which would add another dimension to the company. I'd heard about a business over in Kingston-upon-Thames where they smoked their own salmon, supplied local restaurants, and also had a thriving retail trade. I think the retail shop was doing about £10,000 a week and the annual turnover amounted to about £1.5 or £2 million a year. It was a family business owned by Gordon and Desmond Jarvis, but neither of their sons wanted it. When Gordon retired and Desmond became ill, they approached me in Billingsgate market one day and asked if I would be interested in buying them out – which we did. It was the first business I ever actually bought, and I still have it now. Its value to us at the time was not just the £10,000 or £12,000 the shop was taking each week but that it gave us a retail outlet of our own, along with a ready-made list of 30 or 40 new clients that we could service direct from the shop.

This was in 1993, and by now we were buying a lot of fish from France. I needed an insider on my team to deal with the French. So I did something really cheeky – though looking back on it after everything that happened since, it is quite a funny story. I had been an admirer of the chef, Christian Delteil, for quite a while. He was one of the top chefs, and had his own fine dining restaurant down in Battersea. He had already got one Michelin star and was close to getting his second. But he was in the position that a few of the Michelin restaurants had got into during the recession. They were expensive to run, and the trend in eating had moved away from them to the big People's Palace-style brasseries opened by people like Terence Conran. So Christian wasn't doing so well, and I persuaded him to get out of the kitchen completely. I convinced him to shut down his Battersea restaurant and come over to work at Cutty's. Christian is one of the most inspiring guys I have ever worked with. He's a very tough no-nonsense guy, but he's also got a wonderful sense of humour.

And of course, with what happened next, Christian turned out to be the best new signing Cutty's could possibly have made. The obvious reasons for wanting Christian on board were his expertise and the fact that he was French, and I respected him – but I wonder if I wasn't already thinking at the back of my mind what a great head chef he would be for a Cutty's fish restaurant? Because it was at about this time that Ronnie and I started to daydream about opening our own restaurant. At this time we were doing so much more for the top restaurants and hotels than just supplying them with fish. We were training their young chefs in how to cut fish properly and economically. We were giving advice on menu planning that would work round the best seasonal produce available. They were almost getting a complete restaurant consultancy service – and I'm sure that without knowing it, we contributed quite a lot to people's gross profits at that period. Ronnie was saying things like, 'the amount of consultancy we are doing we might just as well have our own restaurant'. Then somehow or other, it turned from a pipe dream into being the next big thing we were going to do.

It would be a huge step though, because we didn't just want some little neighbourhood eatery. We wanted to open a big budget-busting restaurant that would be massive, and that everybody would be talking about. It became my ambition to do a restaurant version of what I had done with Cutty's. The team was already partly in place. Obviously Ronnie and I were the prime movers: it would be a fish restaurant opened by the two top fishmongers in London. We had Jeremy looking after finance. And we had a real star in Christian as head chef. I knew I had nearly everything I needed to open a huge ground-breaking restaurant. From 1993, when Ronnie and I were first talking about it, we put a hell of a lot of thought into what we wanted to do, and we reckoned we had nearly everything. I would source great produce; Ronnie had fantastic taste buds; Christian was a wonderful chef; and Jeremy was an entrepreneurial money man. But what we didn't have was a site.

Finding the perfect place for our dream restaurant was rapidly becoming a nightmare. Then we got a call from our bank manager at NatWest. He wanted to tell us about these two large branches NatWest had on opposite sides of Kingsway. They didn't need two banks right next to each other so they were going to close one. I went up to have a look, and they were great – two big corner sites in the heart of WC2. So I phoned the German company who actually owned the freeholds, and when they advertised the site as vacant, I was able to register an interest. Then, almost overnight, I got the call to come and pitch for the lease-hold to turn the site into a restaurant. But it was all happening so fast, and I only had 24 hours to put my presentation together, including what the restaurant would look like and everything. The only restaurant designer that I had really heard of was Julian Wickham, because he had designed Corney and Barrow, where I had worked. But he had also done two very trendy restaurants: Kensington Place and the Fifth Floor at Harvey Nichols. So he was a very hot architect/designer. I just rang him up anyway. I think Julian was a bit taken aback by how upfront I was when I asked him to do the presentation with me, but I didn't have any alternative. There wasn't time to do anything but go in and blag it. He said: 'I'll do it. But there's one condition. If you get the deal, you let me design the restaurant.'

I remember the presentation was on a Friday – it must have been in May or June. I turned up in my white fishmonger's coat, stinking of fish as always. I went up the stairs to the board room and there's this very smartly dressed German guy in his 40s. I was 30 then, and I knew this was a family property business, so the guy in front of me was worth billions, literally billions. I just thought, well, I'd better get on with it. But somehow I wasn't intimidated. I don't think I'd had the chance to get worked up, although I might have if I'd had more time to think about it. And also, for me, what gave me confidence was that I firmly believed Cutty's was the best supplier of fine produce in the country. Plus I believed equally in the idea that I had in my mind. I hadn't had time to put anything on paper, but the Germans liked the presentation, and we heard they really did fancy our project. Seven days later we got the call: 'Yes, they liked your presentation, but a large chain, Regent Inns, had been successful in getting the lease.'

It was such a gut-wrenching disappointment. I had been so convinced we were going to get it, that the restaurant we imagined would really work and become a reality. And then for some mass-market catering outfit to get it, felt like a kick in the teeth. But that only lasted for a week, because ten days later the agent was on the phone again. This time he explained that Regent were dragging their heels, so if I could come up with £250,000 the next working day for a deposit on the lease, we could have it.

Finding the £250,000, even at such short notice, wasn't a problem. Cutty's could easily fund that. But now we really did have a project and we had to get serious. So we set up a company, which we called Bank Restaurant Group – because we had already decided the restaurant would be called Bank. I invited Michel Roux to be one of the non-executive directors, because Michel was one of the important people who really gave me my start as a fishmonger. When I got the Waterside Inn at Bray, one of the top restaurants in the whole country, that was what took Cutty's to another level. So giving him that position was a way of recognizing that. It didn't hurt the public relations side of things either to have such a famous chef on board, but really we were saying thank you. Shortly after we'd appointed him, another of our non-execs, Brian Whitford, won an MBE for his contributions to health and safety in the catering industry – which was very amusing when you think of my attitude to health and hygiene and so on over the years. We also had a great financial guy from the City, Stephen Barclay, on the board, so we had put together a good business team. Now we needed to sort out the money.

We budgeted the whole project at £2.4 million and we obviously approached our bank, NatWest, for the loan. Ronnie and I worked out we could put in a million of our own money but first we had to give them evidence of our resources. We discovered that on Cutty's debtor book alone, we were owed £1.5 to £2 million on turnover. That meant we were millionaires on paper at least.

But even as that was still sinking in, it suddenly didn't seem that much money after all. I was going, 'Can we do it? Have we got the money?' Sometimes even Jeremy Omerod didn't know quite where the money was coming from. And NatWest was nervous too. They were bothered because the restaurant market was still very uncertain generally. But in the end they agreed to go to £1.6 million. I think it was partly because one of the NatWest guys, Brian Jeeves, was an old friend of Jeremy and he was on our side. Finally we got the funding sorted out. All the pieces were in place.

The next thing was finding a contractor. I tracked down a building contractor who was more of a shop fitter really, but to this day I have never seen a better builder. Pat Carter was a fabulous builder, brilliant. I had come across him because he had done a restaurant called The Avenue, in Mayfair, on St James's, and I had always admired the restaurant. The chef that opened The Avenue was Enda Flanaghan – an Irish boy and a great cook. Enda became a close friend, and as we got started with the fit-out later he used to come down in the evenings and help us after they had finished serving at the The Avenue. I invited Patrick Carter over to Kingsway to look at the site and see whether he thought he could do it. He took a walk round, and he was like me, an instinctive pricer. He said, 'It will come in around a million.' So I said: 'Build it for £900,000', and we shook hands on that.

This was in the late July or early August of 1995, but the builders wouldn't be going in until December, because we still had a hell of a lot to do. This was where Julian Wickham came in. Using an architect of his prominence turned out to be a really good move. Julian and I certainly had our screaming matches over the next few months, but he was brilliant. At the time I hadn't really taken on board just how much weight he carried in his profession and with the press, so I never took him that seriously – which was probably the best thing I could have done, because we have ended up doing three or four restaurants together. From the point of view of opening our first restaurant though, Julian's clout in the industry was really important. To open a restaurant the size of Bank successfully you have to get to everybody interested, the whole industry.

Christian Delteil designed the kitchen. Of course what he came up with had to be different. His cooking area was the longest one-piece stove in the world. We had it custom-built by a French specialist manufacturer, Bonnet. They needed this huge tower crane to lift it in through the old banking hall windows. All the traffic had to be stopped to get the crane in, so they did it very early one Sunday morning. I remember going up to watch, and thinking, that's one hell of a crane. But actually the kitchen was the least of our problems. The big difficulty was the bank vaults below the old banking hall, which we had planned to turn into all the back office facilities. But because they had been vaults the walls were very solid – two or three feet thick. Getting it knocked through to create a 4,000 square feet back-of-house area was a nightmare. The actual restaurant itself would be 8,000 square feet – absolutely massive for the time. We had a huge air conditioning requirement, but Jeremy was able to work us a good financial arrangement on that. We bought the air conditioning units outright through a company, and installed them on the roof to service the whole building. Then the restaurant leased back the air conditioning services. I was far more concerned about the creative side of starting a new restaurant, but getting the right financial servicing in place is vital. A lot of the equipment we were able to fund through similar lease-back deals.

For me though, the real excitement was planning what Bank would be like as a restaurant. I was confident. The whole thing just felt right. When the builders went in and the hoardings went up, we had them painted with images of what the restaurant would look like. That really got the pulse racing, to see it all starting. But I knew there was going to be no happy medium about this project. It would either be a massive success or we would have crashed and lost everything. I wasn't nervous though. I was so hands-on that it didn't give me time to fret over 'what ifs'. And the driving force for me was that I had such a strong vision of what I wanted it to be like. I could see this big horseshoe bar where everybody would be sitting and having a drink before or after their meal. And there would be some people eating at the bar as well. On a busy night in the restaurant there would be an extra 30 covers on the bar. Over the years I had noticed that it is very rare for a successful restaurant also to have a really good bar – and the same with bars, which don't often do great food. Only in a very few places do you see them both work. But that was what I wanted for Bank.

The bar needed to be the hub of the action. It would be a trendy bar to go to – a place where you would start your evening. But then the boys would start cooking, the service starts. Some of those smells would waft across and the people having a couple of drinks would be thinking, Christ, smell that, lovely. Wallop – you could probably count on 70 or 80 chance customers a day just on that. It was about atmosphere as well. Certainly having a bar area you could eat at meant more covers, but I remembered when I used to go out with friends drinking it was very difficult to get the all-round experience of an evening just at one venue. Instead it would be you met somewhere for a drink with friends, and then you go on and eat, then perhaps go somewhere else afterwards. Denys and

I often used to go out with Ronnie and his wife Michelle, and we used to struggle for somewhere to go for a drink. Then we'd go for a meal, but if you wanted a drink afterwards, you were stuck with where to go again. But we owe Terence Conran a lot, because he more or less pioneered the move away from that to creating a place with a lot of atmosphere that was a one stop shop in terms of your evening out. When the likes of Quaglino's and Langans opened, eating there was an event in itself. And then you had somewhere like Pont de la Tour, where after your meal you could go and sit in the bar and the piano player would still be playing until one or two in the morning, it's fabulous.

This was just the kind of happening feeling I wanted for Bank, and ultimately it was through working with Julian Wickham that I achieved it. Julian and I developed a great relationship – though not necessarily an easy one! I found him really frustrating a lot of the time. He was a nightmare to do business with. Julian was forever in litigation. He was always suing Harvey Nichols or Harvey Nichols was suing him. Even at the time when I went to knock on Julian's door to ask for his help, to be perfectly honest, I wasn't a great lover of his work. The Fifth Floor at Harvey Nichols I thought was okay, and I actually didn't like Kensington Place much. It was too simple for me. In fact I thought the whole restaurant, including the food, was seriously overrated. As much as I admire Roly Lee as a cook, I just thought it was all too hyped up. Even Julian's work at Quaglino's I didn't really get. You can walk into Quaglino's and there is that amazing showpiece staircase, just built for the gossip columnists and the paparazzi, and you think wow, fantastic, what a design, what a world champion. But really it never did much for me. Primarily I went to Julian Wickham because I wanted that space at Kingsway so badly and I didn't know anybody else. But once fate had brought us together, working with the man was the best kind of awful. I miss him and those times so much, I really do – just the day-to-day banter, nothing you can pin down and describe. But he was so inspirational.

Everything always had to be a mystery with Julian though. You never knew what the hell was going on. It didn't give me much to get excited about, so I was always quizzing him. I'd be saying: 'This is my restaurant that I'm spending three million quid on and I don't even know what's gonna be in it.' So it was a challenge for me to try and get inside his head and find out what was going on. But just having a conversation with Julian was quite mentally taxing because he was such a brilliant architect. I felt like a schoolboy, asking him the most simple and mundane questions. It felt like being a little boy at Christmas, trying to find out where your presents were and fishing round your mum and dad's bedroom for them – and the same feeling that even though it was going to take the edge off Christmas Day, you just had to find out what was going on!

I remember sitting down with Julian one evening, and we were nine-parts pissed. We were talking about a feature for the restaurant. It needed a stand-out, conversation piece, like the staircase at Quags. At this stage, the money was rapidly creeping up to the £2 million we'd allowed, and I was trying to get out of Julian what the feature was going to be – and, of course, how much it was going to cost. We did have talking points already, like the kitchen itself, with the record-breaking stove. Also we had a lot of exposed RSJs that looked quite exciting. But I still wanted something that would be totally mind-blowing. So we were sitting there, in the bar of the Waldorf Hotel, which is just across the road from Bank, and we were drinking, of all things, grappa – you might just as well go to a garage and start drinking out of the petrol pump! Anyway Julian finally spoke up, and he said: 'Can you imagine the belly of a whale. I've got the image of a blue whale in my mind, a great whale floating through space.'

I was pretty mystified, and ready to put it down to the grappa talking, but I went along with it, again probably due to the grappa. It turned out that it was a shape he was trying to describe. What he had in mind was something like the hull of a boat, that shape of the framework of the bottom of a boat. And he wanted to hang that shape from the ceiling of the restaurant as a kind of chandelier. I was still trying to get my head round it – and thinking about what this might to do the budget. I said, 'Well, what are you gonna build it in?' And he said, 'Oh, I'll probably do it in wood, slats of wood like in shipbuilding.' Then he added, as if it was an afterthought, 'Or maybe I'll do it in glass.' Immediately I'm thinking that's going to be another quarter of a million quid on the budget. But then I thought: what the fucking hell, you know; I'm going let this man build what he wants to build. It's my restaurant and I'm going to let this brilliant designer express himself. So, still nine parts pissed, we came to the decision that it would be glass.

Then it was time for the hangover. Julian came back and had a meeting with me and Ronnie and Jeremy and Christian to explain what I had agreed to, and he said: 'It's going to take three and a half thousand pieces of glass, all individually cut.' Then the evening all came back to me vividly and I asked all the questions that most boring people who are about to spend thousands on an idea ask. But I never regretted it, and it was surprising, the way it came together. When the glass eventually turned up every piece was different. So it was unbelievably technical, yet at the same time it was so simple putting it together. Going to the kitchen at

Bank we had a glass walkway, and on that glass wall there was an etching of the plan of the chandelier that we actually used to put it together – it's still there now. I remember us all being there in the restaurant late at night putting it up. My dad had come down to help. Enda Flanaghan had come over from The Avenue, and we were all in there hanging the glass at midnight – all because of this wild idea Julian had had, and I'd been there at its conception over a bottle of grappa and a severe hangover.

Julian was someone I could really relate to and in fact our relationship got even better once he stopped working for me directly. Unfortunately, these days what I'm doing within the industry doesn't have an opening for Julian's skills so I don't see so much of him. That's a shame. It was one of those relationships where you don't realize exactly how much you value it until it's gone. Partly I suppose because we were all under so much pressure at the time. We were supposed to open in August, but things ran over and ran over. And then we went over budget. NatWest got very nervous indeed about it. Even though we'd been with them so long, they turned round and let us down. In the spring of 1996 they suddenly pulled the plug. We had gone to them to ask to take the loan up to £2 million to cover things like the over-run and the chandelier. But they just turned round and said, no to the extra £400,000, we aren't funding you any more. It was the difference between ply board on the ceiling and hand-cut glass. For me it was crucial. You don't buy a Saville Row suite and then pull on a pair of wellies with it – and by this stage I wasn't prepared to compromise. But that was their banking decision. They didn't fancy it, end of story.

I'm not the right person to sit in front of a bank manager in any case. With all my enterprises I have never been the kind of man to ask myself 'what if'. I don't think I would have achieved anything like what I have if that had been my attitude. Fortunately I was vindicated, because when Barclays came to see us they were quite happy to put in the extra £400,000 and have an arrangement for £2 million with us. By now, in 1996, interest rates had dropped back down a bit, so it wasn't going to stretch us too badly. Not that I was giving it any thought. I was totally focused on the food and the people who would come to eat. I ignored the financial commitment. Maybe I shouldn't have done that, because Denys and I had just moved to a house in Camden Close in Bickley with a half million pound mortgage. So there were noticeable chunks of money outstanding. But Denys has always been really supportive of all my projects, and she really liked the idea of Bank restaurant. I'm sure she was worried at the time, but she never said a thing to question me.

By now all our family and friends were mucking in at the restaurant, up ladders, hanging glass and whatever needed doing. My dad had a big building contract on at the time and he would send any labourers he could spare over to me. There were loads and loads of us getting stuck in. Pat Carter, the contractor, was still doing the proper build, but the whole family were running around making themselves useful. I remember turning round to Pat and saying, 'I know we've got a contract and I don't want this affecting anything, but I really want this chandelier to go up, can I bring some more people in to help me?' Patrick laughed and said: 'It's your baby. This is your dream; you go for it and the more the merrier. Let's get them all in and let's get this bloody restaurant open.' So we were all working all hours. There was a sandwich bar across on Kingsway we'd go to at odd hours to get some food in. But it wouldn't have bothered me if I'd eaten nothing. As far as I was concerned, stopping for something to eat was time lost. It was five minutes that could have put more of the chandelier up. Five minutes that was not getting the restaurant going. So I used to hate it.

I even used to hate watching the contractors have breaks. Particularly when we had had to postpone the opening from July to September and then again to October, it became one of my pet hates, a kind of obsession. I remember walking onto the site close to the handover and watching all the contractors sit down and have their tea break and their lunch break. I was so frustrated I would be on the phone to Julian, 'What the hell are they stopping for? I thought they were supposed to be accelerating the contract.' He was calm, 'They have to have a break,' and I was shouting the odds, 'They're having a break every two hours.' I was throwing my toys out of the cot, 'Why are you stopping? This is my restaurant isn't it?' Some of the conversations I used to have with Julian were terrible; he must have got off the phone thinking this guy's mad. Maybe I was being unreasonable, but I was so keyed up that I honestly just couldn't fathom out why anyone would want to stop for a break.

One night my dad and Enda were doing a stint helping me hang the glass pieces – it was really close to the opening date in October. We stopped about midnight and went round to the office to close up. By that time I'd upgraded from a Porsche to a Ferrari, which I'd left parked outside the office. We discovered someone had smashed the Ferrari's side window and stolen the radio. So Enda put in a temporary window and we all set off home. I drove over Westminster Bridge. But Enda always rode his little scooter everywhere, so he jumped on his little scooter and whizzed off to his place over one of the other bridges further up river. On the bridge a car smashed straight into him and he was killed outright that night. It was an awful, awful thing, and nothing anyone could do. There is still a bronze plaque in the restaurant at Bank in memory of Enda Flanaghan, a wonderful man.

As we got nearer to opening, Ronnie and I were concentrating on what, for me, was the really exciting stuff – what the menu would be like, and who the actual restaurant team would be. For the front of house I desperately wanted Eric Garnier as my maitre d'. He was the front of house for Quaglino's, and I was so impressed with what he achieved there. Luckily he was a friend of Christian Delteil, so he agreed to come and look at the site, and he said yes. Now I needed a number two for Christian in the kitchen, and I had my eye on Tim Hughes at Le Caprice. A lot of people were writing about him at the time, so I targeted him, and I got him! These guys ended up running a staff of around a hundred people. Ronnie and I were also grabbing ideas from everywhere. The team went over to New York for a recce and went to about 70 different restaurants – gleaning an idea here and a dish there.

You can't reinvent the wheel but there were certain dishes that we chose to major on. We were perfectionists about the fish and chips, because as fishmongers it would be our signature dish. So it had to be a perfect Scottish halibut with excellent big, fat, crisp chips. And Christian reinvented some old classics – stuffed cabbage and ox cheek with lentils, hock of pork. A lot of chefs were using offal at the time, Pierre Kauffman, for example, had made his name on pigs trotters. It was a side-effect of the recession that had pushed chefs into making exciting dishes out of cheaper ingredients. It wasn't peasant food, but it was comfort food and the City boys really liked it. Christian Delteil came out with a great line. He said it was 'liberated French,' though it later became known as modern British. The initial menu was my favourite. It was very big and well executed but it had the flexibility that you could have the prix fixee for £12.95 or you could spend £70 or £80 a head.

The restaurant was starting to look good and we were about to open, but then we realized we needed to have a computer system for the bookings, bills, payments and so on. So Jeremy was put in charge of finding the right epos system. We'd decided that another of our innovations would be that everything would be automated, which wasn't the norm then as it is now. Jeremy looked at the market leaders and he also met up with a chap called Dr Ken Stratford. Ken's day job was extremely eminent – he was a Professor of Neurology at Oxford University. But he had an eccentric hobby, which was building computer systems for the restaurant industry. He had built a system for Rick Stein at his restaurant down in Cornwall. When we got the quotes in from the conventional bidders, Jeremy said, 'I think Ken and I can build a cheaper system.' So one thing led to another, and they did build it. It wasn't cheaper, as it happens, but it was a very stable and robust system – and little did we know at the time how important it would become to the company. Because the next thing Ken and Jeremy did was develop it into a reservation system. We had a system that meant we could get the maximum profitability from a 210 cover restaurant. We owned the system and it had the potential to be a separate business. In a way it was just something we had stumbled upon, but ultimately it was to become one of our huge selling points when we went public.

There was a lot of speculation about Bank restaurant before it opened. The whole industry seemed to be talking about us. One of the things that got the restaurant writers interested was that Christian Delteil had been out of the kitchen for nearly three years – and yet he'd been on the verge of his second Michelin star when he closed his restaurant. But we didn't want the press to focus on just one man, or one aspect of Bank. I had seen the dangers of vesting too much PR on individuals. When Gordon Ramsay left the AtoZ restaurant it had been a big blow for them. So it was a team effort and I was very stringent on projecting that. We had poached a very clever PR girl, Kelly Lutchford, from Matthew Freud's company and we started off paying her about £3,000 a month. She had plenty to work with because Bank seemed to be achieving world records at every turn. It had started with Christian's cooking range, which was the longest one-piece stove in Europe. Then the chandelier was a huge talking point – the biggest ever to be installed in a restaurant. I would love to see the statistics now of how many architectural design students came into the restaurant and spent £50 a head for a three course meal, just so they could see the chandelier. And of course, along with the positive publicity, there were a lot of people wanting to rubbish us. People said they weren't sure about the location, but I thought it couldn't be bettered – the City out of one window and Theatreland out of the other.

It seemed like forever, but eventually we reached the end of October 1996, and we were finally ready to open. We started off with a couple of trial nights where we had private parties for friends and family and so on. I was staying at the Waldorf because we were round the clock by then. The night before we opened to the public was Julian Wickham's party, which was really the grand opening, because he had so many influential friends to invite. This was the big one; everyone who was anyone in the industry would be there. So I walked over from the Waldorf to the restaurant. We had just taken the hoardings down that morning. It was dark by the time I went back over, and they had put the lights on in the restaurant. So as I walked towards it I could see in through the lighted windows. And I could see it all, glimpses through the windows – the mural, and the chandelier, and the bar – and it was full of people, you could see them moving about and holding wine glasses. I stopped and stood there on the pavement in the dark, with Bush House and Australia House behind me, looking at my restaurant.

And I just choked up. I thought, fucking hell, look at this place. That's probably the first time I've actually shed tears, standing there outside and looking through those windows and seeing the place. My dream really existed, and Denys and the kids were waiting for me in there. And I just thought, Christ Almighty, look what we've achieved, myself and Ron. The two flash lads, these flamboyant fishmongers, not only had we got the ear of 99 per cent of the top restaurants in the country, but look what we've created now. And 50 or 60 yards away from me, there it was, with the lights blazing, a real beauty. I couldn't go in. I had to turn round and go back to the Waldorf to sort myself out. I went back to the hotel room and sat down on the edge of the bed to pull myself together. I wiped my eyes. When I managed to pull myself together and go into the party, I could tell it was going well. The champagne was going round into the early hours. Towards the peak of the party the original bank manager from NatWest came up to me. He took me aside, and you could see he'd had a fair amount of our champagne, but you know what they say, 'in vino veritas', so he pulled me over and looked at me, and that was when he said: 'Well, you know you'll be skint by February, don't you?'

Chapter Five

Fish Market Meets Stock Market

THE FOLLOWING day, Friday 31ˢᵗ October, was when we opened to the public. Everybody was very stressed. I still had the bank manager's parting shot about going bust ringing in my ears. The boys in the kitchen were feeling the pressure too. We started serving lunch, and we had about 120 people in for lunch – that meant we were about half full, which wasn't bad. In the evening we must have done about 175 for dinner, which again, was okay. That first day we served about 300 people in all, which was alright – but to be honest, it wasn't more than alright. It was like that *Yes, Minister* episode where Jim Hacker wants to know if he is doing alright as a minister and they keep telling him he's doing alright. The following day was the Saturday, the first weekend day, and we did the same again as we had on Friday. Then Sunday was a bit quieter, and Monday about the same.

All the famous restaurant critics had been in to eat the first day we opened – A.A. Gill, Fay Maschler, Jonathan Meades and the rest. But the first review didn't come out until the Tuesday morning. It was in the *Evening Standard*, the London evening paper which hits the streets about 11 o'clock in the morning, in plenty of time for the lunch trade. The review was by Fay Maschler, the *Standard's* highly respected food critic. People in the industry were always trying to get close to Fay. But she understood chefs well because her sister, Beth Coventry, was a chef at Green's, the fashionable Piccadilly fish restaurant. Cutty's had supplied Green's, so Fay had heard a lot about me and Ronnie, and I think she had been interested from the start in what we were up to. So that Tuesday morning at the beginning of November, Fay Maschler's review came out – and we were the first large-scale restaurant she ever gave two stars. From that day everything changed. It went from steady business to phenomenal in the space of 24 hours. Things just went mad. We were serving 650 a day – 250 for lunch and about 400 in the evening, and that was just the people we could get in. We had eight staff doing nothing but answering the phone. Ronnie and I just stood at the door and watched people come pouring in.

We knew Jonathan Meades was going to review us in *The Sunday Times*, but the previous Sunday, our first weekend, we'd looked and there had been no review. I think it was to do with deadlines, but it meant we were waiting a whole week for the review. So when the weekend came round again, and Saturday night we were desperate to see if it would be in, and what he was going to say. Pierre Kauffman had come in for dinner, and we were all of us itching to find out. By the early hours of Sunday morning we knew the paper would be out, so we jumped in a cab and dashed over to one of the main line stations to get hold of an early copy. We were tearing the paper to bits trying to get to the right section, and then we read Jonathan Meades' review, and he'd given us 9/10. It was unheard of, an endorsement like that. Jonathan had always been a big fan of Christian Delteil and he loved everything we were doing at Bank. From then on we never looked back. The lunch trade with the boys popping in from the City and all the law firms, accountants and journalists, was fantastic. Then in the evenings we had all the theatre crowd and people on a night out. We paid everything back to Barclays in just over a year.

And it went on getting better and better. A month later we won the accolade of Restaurant of the Year – an incredible achievement given we'd only been open six weeks. We were the 'it' restaurant the Christmas of '96. I would be standing at reception and there would be a queue of people in the street, trying to come in to eat after the theatre. That was where the big bar area came into its own, just as I had always dreamed it would. I took people over to the bar and got them drinking so they wouldn't mind waiting. And that was exactly how I had hoped it would happen when we originally designed Bank. All my ideas of being a successful bar/restaurant with great food and a fashionable bar were actually working out. It was only a couple of weeks after we had opened that Jeremy said to me, 'You'd better come and sit down so we can talk about the finances.' I was confused because I didn't see how there could be a problem, given the fantastic business we were doing. But in fact it turned out that what he wanted was to discuss what to do with all this money we had coming out of our ears! It was just a matter of months before the initial loan from Barclays was paid back. As things worked out, I never got a chance to stick two fingers up to the NatWest guy. You are too busy getting on with life to worry about the losers who didn't believe in you – all the same it was quite a good feeling knowing that I was proving him wrong.

There was one downside though, which I think at the time we were probably too busy to pay proper attention to. Like any industry, there is quite a bit of the 'green eye' in the restaurant trade. The industry was forced to look at us differently – we'd gone from being basically fishmongers to being restaurateurs, so we were now competitors as well as suppliers. Cutty's started losing a bit of business from some of the chefs. Maybe we were a bit in their faces, these super-rich fishmongers who suddenly opened a mega-trendy, successful restaurant. We were no longer going in at kitchen doors talking to chefs; we were walking up to the front of house and sitting down with restaurant owners, which is a different kind of relationship. There probably was a view that we didn't know our place, and there was a little bit of ill feeling from a few guys. But at the same time a whole new, unexpected, line of business was opening up for us, which oddly enough, was the computer reservation system. A lot of the big restaurateurs who had come in to test the menu thought the food was good – but they thought the reservation system was even better! They started asking about it. Who designed it? Did we own it? And then we got big names like Raymond Blanc and Terence Conran asking to buy it.

We were on the crest of a wave now, and it was gathering speed. It was only a few months later, in 1997, that we were asked if we were interested in looking at a possible restaurant site in Borough Market, just beside the southern end of London Bridge. In those days the Borough area of Southwark was a bit neglected, but it had so much character, with the old fruit and vegetable market under the railway arches, and Southwark Cathedral and all the historic connections with Dickens and Chaucer. I went to look at the site, which was an old pea-shelling factory, and from the first day I saw it I fell in love with it. I went to the lads – Ronnie and Jeremy, and the other guys on the board – and we all really fancied it, so we secured the site. Then the thought process of what we were actually going to do with it kicked in. My big idea was that despite the success of Bank, we were still primarily fishmongers and I wanted to tap into that. Right from the early days I had always been on a mission to get people eating and enjoying the very best fish, and this seemed like the ideal opportunity to do something about it. At this stage Ronnie and I had become almost VIPs within the catering industry. We were these very flamboyant London fish suppliers who had proved we could also hack it as restaurateurs, and that meant a lot of people were beginning to equate us with the top chefs. We had become more or less the voice of prime fish in this country, certainly as far as the hotel and catering industry were concerned. So it was pretty obvious that the new site in Borough Market should be purely a fish restaurant, majoring on serving the very best fish to be had in London.

I knew exactly how I wanted it to be. I had been spending a lot of time thinking about flavours that I used to enjoy when I was a kid, and in my early days in the kitchen and as a fish supplier. I'd been trained classically and I had begun to wonder what had happened to all the classic fish dishes that people really love to eat, that you never seem to see on menus any more. Also about this time we'd all finally had a chance to start going away for the occasional holiday to the Med – the south of France, Portugal, parts of Spain, Italy, Greece – and we'd all been raving to each other about the food. And we'd be saying why can't we get this lovely Mediterranean food at home? We want just a simple piece of grilled fish, a lovely glass of chilled white wine, and a really fresh tasty salad. Why is it that everything in London restaurants is so fucked around with? Because at the end of the day, I think the meals that are memorable, that you enjoy, are really down to timing and how you feel at the time – whether you're relaxed; whether you just want a chilled-out lunch; whether you've got nothing to worry about; rather than thinking about baby sitters, business and the rest. I remember the best meal I ever had was in a little beach bar we would often go to in Portugal. You walk in and it's all very spit and sawdust. There's a tin barbecue and a one-burner stove, but they produce the most amazing grilled fish and the freshest salad you could ever eat. This particular meal was in February. We were sitting looking out, and they had floods over the sand-dunes. There were loads and loads of eels migrating, and the restaurant had caught some of them, so there was a big chunk of marinated eel on the barbecue. And with it we had a perfect salad and perfect chips – big hand-cut home-made chips, crispy on the outside and soft and tasty on the inside. And a bottle of the local wine, just a green one, a vino verde. It was absolutely brilliant.

Obviously not everybody is going to rave about barbecued eel, but it was the whole experience. And I thought, what's happened to this traditional way of eating? What's happened to the old favourites? I love whitebait. I love a good prawn cocktail. One of my personal theories on fish, particularly the well-known white fish like sole and plaice and so on, is that it actually doesn't have a lot of flavour of its own. I think it does have a unique and interesting texture, but I think to bring out what little flavour it has, you have to do the simplest things with it. It's the kind of thing Gary Rhodes sometimes does, something basic but great, like smoked haddock on a Welsh rarebit. The traditional dishes were what I really missed from when I was a child, and I thought other people probably did as well. So that's how I developed the idea of a really first class restaurant where the signature dish was basically a bag of fish and chips. I put all these ideas I had about fish, and about how people like to eat, and I came up with a restaurant that would be accessible to everyone who ever even bought a take-away, but it would be of the highest quality. I imagined a menu that would be very different from Bank's menu, because I wanted it to be somewhere the Duchess and the dustman would sit down together. And I wanted to get kids eating fish as well. With spaghetti bolognaise, why always use beef? Why not have tuna in your bolognaise?

I don't know how confident the others were about it, but I really, really believed in it. I felt that I had taken all these opinions and gripes that people had about what was missing, not only in

London restaurants, but around the whole country. The things everybody agreed were really disappointing, like the fact that if you walked along any one of our sea fronts, you would see fantastic fish being landed, but you never got to eat it. Instead it would be sent off to France, and even in Grimsby you'd be getting frozen fish with your chips. There are some fantastic people working in the fishing industry in this country. Anywhere round the coast of the UK, you will find great fishermen, all the way from Brighton and Hastings, to the Essex flats, all the way up to Lowestoft, all the way around Scotland, Milford Haven down to Wales, and obviously the West Country. Throughout the whole island of Britain we have access to wonderful fish, and I wanted to give people a chance to eat it. And the great thing was, as the leading fish supplier, I was in the perfect position to do it. The beauty of the restaurant project was that it integrated so well into our existing fish supply business. I would be able to go to the market or speak to my coastal suppliers and what was offered on the restaurant menu would slot into place with what was going on in the business generally. Large wholesale orders for the hotel trade would be prepared at Cutty's alongside smaller speciality requirements for the new restaurant. Then the filleted fish would go straight into the kitchen where it wouldn't need a large team of chefs because most of the preparation work would already have been done. The whole thing would be an integrated operation.

The other good point was that this would enable us to make substantial cost savings, which would help achieve the other really important goal of the restaurant: that it had to be affordable. I was looking more at Pizza Express's prices than I was at LiveBait's prices. There was always going to be the option that a certain kind of client could come in and have grilled lobster and chips and a bottle of Chablis for £40 a head, but you would also be able to get two courses and a glass of wine for £15 a head. It all came together so quickly. I remember Ronnie and I sitting down and we wrote the menu in a couple of hours. We came up with the tuna burger for the kids. We had a club sandwich with sword-fish instead of chicken. We substituted grilled smoked salmon for bacon. All those ideas that got so talked about, we came up with in a few hours – and a lifetime as well, of course, because it was what we'd always been about. And that was how Fish! restaurant came into being.

The concept for Fish! was brilliant, but that didn't make it any easier to turn it into reality. We needed to raise £2 million, not just for Fish! in Borough Market, but also to make it the flagship of what we hoped would eventually become a chain of fish res-taurants in the South East. With the figures Jeremy was coming up with from Bank, and the success of the reservation system, flo-tation had obviously already become a possibility. Now we knew the time was right – that was how we would raise the money to start Fish!. We were introduced to some brokers and we went for Beeson Gregory. I wanted to do six Fish! restaurants to start with, and I presented that plan to the City. I projected that we would open the restaurants in and around the M25 area and that they would generate £125,000 a year. Bank was making £1.3 million at the time. It was a healthy profit projection. We only released 11 per cent of the company's shares but that raised us the £2 million easily when we had the initial flotation in March 1998. What the City was looking at was predominantly a successful fishmongers with one extremely profitable restaurant and some big plans. With the fishmongers side being about 40 per cent of our business we looked to be a good bet and we floated with an excellent rating.

So we had the capital we needed, but with it came a new pressure, which we hadn't had before, from the City itself. We had all these new investors on board, and of course they wanted to see things happening pretty quickly. They were pushing us to get this first Fish! restaurant, in Borough Market, open as soon as possible. But the Borough Market site was owned by a bunch of trustees, so they weren't typical landlords at all, and that was making things difficult for us. We eventually convinced them to give us the lease. In fact I think we won them over. For example, they originally wanted the site, the pea-shelling factory, to be split into 90 per cent retail and 10 per cent restaurant but we went ahead and made it 90 per cent restaurant. Oddly enough they never challenged us on it. I think Fish! did so much for the area as a whole that they accepted it as a fait accompli. Even with the trustees coming round, we still had English Heritage on our backs because of the conservation aspect. The area of Borough Market is very historical, and they wanted to preserve that – but at the same time we had Julian Wickham trying to build us a fish restaurant for £650,000. We had planned to open in August 1998, but it soon became obvious that all the red tape we were facing was going to make that date impossible.

Fish! was such a different experience from starting Bank. There were a whole different set of issues. Bank was like a special private dream for Ronnie and me and the team. We knew from the start that it would be an all-or-nothing project, because we had to convince the rest of the world of what we were doing. So with Bank we risked breaking the budget because it was so much more important for us to do something special that would attract the attention of everyone – the restaurant industry, the architecture and design world, the journalists. But when it came to Fish!, we had already established our reputation, and now we were a public company, with shareholders to answer to, so staying as close as possible to the budget was much more important. But some things did work in our favour. With the design, for example, we were already halfway there because the old pea-shelling factory was such a unique building, Julian Wickham designed a kitchen and a bar area. We planned it along 'diner' lines with a big walking stick shaped bar and a theatre kitchen. At Bank of course, Christian Delteil had needed a large technical kitchen, but the requirements at Fish! were much more straightforward. Because it was basically just fish, with various different sauces and garnishes, we didn't need to build an all-singing, all-dancing kitchen. The kitchen at Fish! was designed to serve a minimum of 200 covers a day, yet only takes about five chefs to run it – and eventually it ended up serving nearly 600 people a day. It's highly functional, and from a business point of view, very cost-effective.

All the same, with all the conservation regulations and liaising with the different committees, it was inevitable that we got behind schedule, which meant I had to do some talking to the brokers. Basically what we had to offer our shareholders was two different restaurant brands. Bank was already proven, but was not the kind of restaurant you could open just anywhere. It was very much a big city centre style of restaurant. Then there was Fish!, as yet unproven, but with the potential to go out into the suburbs, certainly throughout the South East, and possibly even end up as a franchise. I think this is where life can become difficult for an entrepreneur, no matter what area you are in. You personally have a very clear idea of what your brand should be and what its strengths are, but the investors may not share your vision, or they get cold feet and want some quick returns, so they end up trying to dilute the brand. Looking back I feel this was probably already beginning to happen to us, even at this early stage. What happened was that the City wanted more restaurants, and they wanted them next week, not next month and certainly not next year.

The brokers thought there was mileage in a suburban version of Bank, so that materialized as the next project. There was a restaurant at Number One, Lawn Terrace, in Blackheath in south London. The owner contacted us to see if we would be interested in buying it. It was a passable local brasserie, and the pressure from the brokers was mounting, so we decided to buy it. We put in a version of the Bank menu and re-branded the restaurant under the name Lawn, and it became a pretty good suburban version of Bank. It was quite successful, but we still hadn't got Fish! open. We had number two restaurant up and running before what I felt was the much more important project: the Fish! chain.

Another slight problem was that while Julian was the perfect designer to be working with our very personal team of friends on Bank, he probably wasn't ideal to be communicating with a plc. Probably the only thing that was keeping Julian on board was me. He and I have always had a great relationship, but no one else seemed to be able to work with him. The other directors were already beginning to fall into the plc mode of thinking, where all they were thinking about was 'Can we open it on budget? And can we keep to schedule?' Even then, and this was only late '98, early '99, you could see that this very rigid business outlook was setting in. It wasn't at all the same attitude we had with Bank, not the same questions. With Bank it was always, 'how amazing can we make it?' whereas with Fish! they wanted the numbers.

I believe that what Julian achieved at Fish! was actually much cleverer than what he did with Bank. With Fish! he created a restaurant where you had five chefs cooking and ten waiters on the floor and could do 600 people a day. I think that was a much tougher assignment than Bank. Bank was the luxurious, all-encompassing brasserie where he had an almost open-ended budget – but Julian actually built Fish! for only £650,000. Julian is such a natural, instinctively brilliant designer. Even though he didn't get on so well with the board, to this day I would love to do something with Julian again. Hopefully I will wake up one morning and have a wacky idea to do my own place in London with 700 seats and see if I could fill it. That would be when I would call Julian. Not even for the project, really – I don't think it would quite matter if we never got open, if we never did anything. It would just be to have those evenings again sitting down talking complete bollocks to each other. The meetings we have had where we achieved absolutely nothing that you could quantify in business terms.

But he could be exasperating. He used to love to come and eat in Bank, and later in Fish!, and he loved fish and chips – but never the way it was on the menu. We'd have a lovely fresh piece of Scotch halibut, but Julian wanted Dover sole and chips – completely messed the whole kitchen up. Julian wanted the Dover sole and he'd want it filleted and then put in the same shape as we served the halibut so it looked like normal fish and chips, except, of course it was Dover sole. Julian was Christian's cross to bear. After we'd got the restaurants open, Julian came back to haunt him, and I remember watching Christian's face: 'Now he wants the Bank fish and chips, but no, with him it must be Dover sole.' At the time he drove us mad, but when I look back on those days now, it was so exciting. Life moves on, and you don't realize what an adventure it was until afterwards. I get a bit emotional about it. It's sad to think that Bank is separate now, and it's not the old team any more. I think letting go of that part of the business was probably one of the worst decisions I ever made.

Once we got into the build on Fish! though, I was really focused on it. The project was so important to me. And I had a massive stroke of luck in PR terms. I was asked to do a television documentary. It was called *Fish Tales*, by a documentary maker called Neil Green, all about Billingsgate Market. Neil approached three people who were heavily involved in the market, and the buyer he wanted to follow was me. We filmed all through the autumn into November. I remember there were some great evening shots we did of me at the building site for Fish! in Borough Market – all atmospheric, with the darkness gathering and the lights coming on under the arches. Fish! was very much my baby. I had told the directors how I wanted it to be, and I projected to them a turnover of about £25,000 a week, more than a million a year, on which we could make around a hundred grand profit. Nothing special, but a starting point, and the directors said: 'This one is Tony's' and let me run with it. Just as Neil Green was finishing filming, the news came out that I had been nominated for the Entrepreneur of the Year on the AIM (Alternative Investment Market). He asked if he could film the awards ceremony, and we went along – and I won it! I couldn't believe it. Fish! was due to open in early February 1999, and the Thursday before, the documentary, *Fish Tales*, went out on television. That show was watched by 9.5 million people, and Fish! opened the following Saturday, and we did 600 covers on the first day.

It was unbelievable advertising. It was such luck. So we are at the beginning of February 1999 and it took off straight away.

There were a couple of little things on the menu that weren't practical. Perhaps the cold langoustine with mayonnaise was a bit difficult because you could only get them when the weather was good. And the way the menu worked, centred totally around what was the good fish that day, which took a bit of getting used to for some people. But basically it worked, especially the classics. I had a fantastic compliment from Andrew Lloyd Webber on the day we opened. He'd been to Le Caprice and The Ivy during the week and they told him that whitebait wasn't available, not in season, but we had fantastic whitebait, which he wrote about. But it did cut both ways a bit, because of course, as a fishmonger, I was supplying the Caprice and the Ivy! The main thing though, was that Fish! achieved everything I wanted, and more. When it came to the reviews, the usual suspects came in and they were all very kind. Hugh Fearnley-Whittingstall gave us a fantastic review and two of the big reviews used a word that really blew me away. When I read it, it made me feel so proud. They used the word, uncritisizeable, which to me was fantastic.

The turnover that I had projected to the City for Fish! was between £20,000 and £25,000 a week, but the next thing we knew we were turning over more like £75,000 a week, still with the same number of chefs. I think the success of Fish! was down to a number of things coming together at one moment. All the favourable press coverage we had was very helpful. We were in the financial media because of the flotation of the company, and the food press was very excited about the first specialist fish restaurant from the top fish supplier. Then of course, there was the huge number of people who watched the television documentary a few nights before we opened. So the public awareness on all fronts was just unparalleled. The PR campaign was unbelievable;

money doesn't buy that kind of coverage. I think in the first year of Fish!, the lead up to the opening and the six months afterwards, we must have had more than 500 press cuttings. And when it came down to it, Fish! did live up to all the hype. It was great food, a groundbreaking concept, and a very healthy menu as well, at a time when everybody was becoming much more aware of nutrition. It is the kind of place you can go with your friends and have a great evening without breaking the budget or the diet.

Looking back over my career, there have been three real significant moments, where I have taken a moment to stand back and say to myself, 'Yes, I have actually achieved what I wanted' and doing Fish! was definitely one of them. The first one though, had come quite a few years before, when Ronnie and I opened the new fish processing unit at the back of the Old Kent Road. I looked at that place when we had just finished it, and I just found it unbelievable that we were responsible for something that good. It was so well-designed, like a surgery almost, you would have been happy to have your tonsils out on our fish filleting benches! It was that state-of-the-art. I know it's hard to get excited about a fish factory, but to me it was beautiful. And we had laid this blue tile floor with the Cutty's logo in it, and we had every top chef down in this chilled room, about 180 people, and we were serving them oysters and champagne and showing them this state of the art fishmongers; that was a fantastic time for me, I thought that was brilliant.

I pretty much pinched myself and thought, 'Bloody hell, look at this place.' But you can't dwell on it for long because you are driven by the fact that you have to make it work. So it was a slightly different feeling from when we opened Bank. I will never forget that moment when they had just taken down the hoardings from outside and you could actually see into the restaurant for the first time. With Cutty's it was just Ronnie Truss and me on our own, and so you always had this awareness, 'I've got to make this work now, the business depends on me.' With Bank there was more of a sense of having achieved something lasting. I thought to myself well if we never serve another customer from this day, no one can take this moment away from me. This is it, I've done it, I've achieved it. Oddly enough I wasn't desperately worried about whether it would become a famous restaurant. Obviously I wanted it to work and be financially viable, but I didn't envisage what would actually happen – that Bank would build a reputation and have an impact on the industry.

But when that did happen with Bank, that brought it home to me what could be done, which I think directly influenced the way I went about doing Fish!. And opening Fish! was definitely the third defining moment in my career. I think it was so special to me because it was so personal. I had this idea close to my heart that it would be possible to make a success with a very simple restaurant serving wonderful fresh fish cooked in a straightforward way. I just instinctively knew that was what people wanted, but it had been hard to persuade the money men of that, so when I was proven right, that was a good feeling. I had pushed for it and put my own reputation on the line, and it bloody well worked.

The next big thing for us as a company though, was to capitalize on the epos system – and this was where the financial guys were able to shine. Quite rapidly after the opening of Bank we had begun supplying epos and reservation systems to hotels and restaurant groups. This side of the business was doing really well. There was a great wave of new computer systems-based business at this time, and we were riding the crest of that wave. So we

decided it was time to bring it into the main plc, Bank Group Restaurants. We nominally paid £250,000, but it was really more of
an accounting exercise to tidy up the loose ends, a paper for paper
transaction. But it was growing so fast that by the beginning of
2000 it became obvious the computer business could stand on
its own feet as a separate company. So in April we demerged it
from the main company and floated it in its own right. This new
company, purely covering the systems we had created, was called
Quadranet. And it floated for £26 million. We had bought it in for
£250,000 and got it away in about nine months for £26 million.
We all made a lot of money on that deal – Ronnie Truss, Jeremy
Omerod, myself, and other board members and investors. We'd
all become millionaires. There is no doubt, a lot of people made a
lot of money on the Quadranet transaction. No wonder the City
thought I had golden bollocks.

And it was an extraordinary time. It was this kind of dream
where I just couldn't put a foot wrong. The restaurants, Bank
and Fish!, were doing phenomenally, and then Quadranet – it
seemed as though everything I touched turned to gold. There was
a funny example of that. A few days after the Quadranet float,
Vinnie Jones invited me to go up to Liverpool with him to watch
the Grand National. I'd met Vinnie briefly when I was building
Fish! and he was filming *Lock, Stock and Two Smoking Barrels* on
location at Borough Market. But we didn't get to know each other
properly until the following Christmas when we were holidaying
with our families in Barbados. Vinnie and I became firm friends,
so off I went on the train with him up to the National, though I'm
not into racing. We had John Ward the gun maker with us and the
footballers, Jo Kinnear and John Hartson and we couldn't move
for autograph hunters, so in the end the Aintree people found a

little box for us. They provided us with a bit of a bar, but the only drawback was that we couldn't get to the bookies to put our bets on. Vinnie solved that by being our bookmaker and we were all betting with him. By the last race we'd obviously all had a few drinks, and this last race was the kind of thing nobody would bet on who knew anything about racing – it was a hurdle for amateur lady jockeys. But I didn't know anything about racing, so I was going to have a bet, and there was a horse called Quadraco. With what had just happened with Quadranet it was the obvious choice, even though it was a rank outsider – 58 to 1. I grabbed everything I had in my pocket which was about £50 and put £25 of it on each way on with Vinnie and another £25 each way with another guy. And I got someone to phone through to Corals to put £600 on it each way. Needless to say, with the way my luck was then, it won! It was my first serious bet on a horse and I worked it out I had won about £37,000. So we all piled back into the train back down to Euston, and we all started playing cards, and almost inevitably I won about another £7,000 off everyone at cards. I was riding this most incredible high that had lasted about two years, from the opening of Bank. It was as though I only had to think of something for it to succeed beyond my dreams. It wasn't a dream though; fate really was throwing all this money at me.

But fate had something else in store for me as well, that was going to turn my life from a dream into a nightmare. It had started back in 1998, at the time we first floated our company. At exactly the moment where everything was starting to go fantastically, unbelievably right, a train of events had been set in motion that would eventually make my life, and my family's lives, a misery. A journalist from the *Daily Mirror* had come to interview me about Bank being named Restaurant of the Year and the initial public offering of the company on the market. We'd been chatting about all the characters in the restaurant industry and I was telling her anecdotes about some of the top chefs. I happened to mention a story Marco Pierre White had told me about a particularly irritating lady eating at his restaurant and how – so he had told me – he'd ended up lacing her squid ink risotto with real ink. It was just one of those little stories you tell when journalists are looking for a bit of colour, and I said something like 'He put real ink in it'. Although it was obvious from the context, what I didn't exactly say in so many words, was that this was a story Marco had told me. But anyway the journalist went off happy and I thought nothing more about it. I never even saw the article when it came out in the *Mirror*, because the family and I were grabbing a quick break in Portugal.

I got back home and went into the office to go through the paperwork – we were only a couple of weeks from the float. There was all the normal junk that builds up on your desk while you are away, and among it was a solicitor's letter. I picked it up and gave it a look over. I couldn't make any sense of it at first. It didn't seem like anything that could be addressed to me, because it was all about libel. Then the words began to strike home. It was from solicitors acting on behalf of their client, Mr Marco Pierre White. It was all a bit of a blur as I looked at it, but two phrases leapt out at me. They were: 'His good name' and 'substantial damages'.

Chapter Six

Three Little Words

S O THERE it was. The celebrity chef and restaurateur, Marco Pierre White, was suing his old friend the well-known fishmonger and restaurateur, Tony Allan, for libel. There wasn't much prospect of keeping that out of the press while the flotation of my company was happening. I don't suppose Marco would ever have wished to be libelled – just as I never wanted to make the slip of words that I did. But if I was going to get sued for libel, it was very bad timing. The crap hit the fan in the press just a few days after the date of our initial public offering on the market. I don't know who put out the press releases about it, but it certainly wasn't me. Marco, who had taken the initiative to sue, was the one in the driving seat – while I was now chairman of a plc, and had a board to answer to. With the boards of public companies being notoriously averse to risk, it was a pretty safe bet at the time that there would be pressure from the board to settle the action out of court. And you only had to look at the newspaper for the share prices to see that there was likely to be money available to do that.

A lot of this was going through my mind as I looked at the letter. I was thinking, 'For God's sake, what's all this about? Marco's a mate; I would never say anything to make him look bad. He knows that, why is he suing me?' Because Marco was an old friend. We had first met way back in 1988, and I had been supplying him with fish for about ten years. We had got to know each other so well in that time – our families were friends and we all used to go out together. Back then both of us were these young mavericks making our way in our respective careers and we had a lot in common. Marco would always be on the phone, and we'd have long talks into the early hours. My first daughter, Charlie, was just a toddler, and Denys had not long had Holly, our second daughter. I think it used to drive Denys mad when she had just got the two children settled down and then the phone would go and it would be Marco. But Marco wasn't really in a steady relationship, so he would be telling me all about how his girlfriend had left him and what was going on. I was a listening ear, and in his turn he was doing the same for me in business terms – Cutty's owed a lot of its reputation to Marco's support. But it was always a two-way process with us. I supplied him with bloody good fish and I bent over backwards for Marco in lots of ways. We had spent a lot of quality time together over the years.

I suppose the big difference between Marco and me was that I was much more settled than him. I had Denys and the children, and as a fishmongers, Cutty's wasn't so dependent on fashion and trends in eating as Marco was as an individual opening restaurants. He knew there would always be people in the industry ready to have a go at him. As I have found myself, the British aren't too keen on success. Maybe Marco was feeling threatened by what was happening with me and Cutty's and the restaurants. If I look at it from his point of view, it was just the kind of situation that would make you feel insecure. Here's this guy you have known for ages who sells you fish. He's a mate but he certainly isn't going to cramp your style or steal your thunder as a chef. Then suddenly – almost overnight – he's opened this massive, award-winning celebrity restaurant, he's become Entrepreneur of the Year, and he's about to float his company on the market. For someone with Marco's personality, all that could be very hard to swallow. But it was a very, very sad thing for me all the same. I would never have thought that that was how two mates would end up. All that honour and loyalty that we had built up had gone out of the window. Unfortunately, if you succeed in business that is one of the hard lessons you have to learn. It was really my first proper experience of that, so I was very disappointed – but maybe not totally surprised that something like that had happened. But Marco would be sure to regret it and change his mind the next day. The trouble was, once the lawyers are involved, things take on their own momentum, regardless of the individuals concerned.

As soon as I had understood that the letter was deadly serious, and this was really happening, my first reaction was disbelief that I had actually said anything libellous about Marco – I had certainly never meant to. So I phoned my PR girl, Kelly Lutchford, and she said, 'I will get on to the *Mirror* and check it out.' She was back on the phone again all too quickly, saying, 'Yes, it's on the tape. That's exactly what you said. You should have said, "*Marco told me* he had put ink in"'. So there was no wriggling with that – just three words forgotten, and that was it. It was one of the first big interviews I had done for the national press, and I hadn't realized how careful you have to be. I understand now why a lot of famous businessmen won't let any interview be printed unless they have had a chance to read it back first. A lot of American entrepreneurs insist on having their press people and even a lawyer present throughout interviews. I'm not sure I would go that far, but it's certainly something to be aware of – especially once you become financially worth suing! I was unlucky in another way as well, because Piers Morgan, then the editor of the *Daily Mirror*, and Marco were good friends, so the *Mirror* was a paper Marco read.

At the time I didn't really take on board just how serious a libel action is. As I was to discover, many libel cases are tried at the High Court in the Strand, London, in front of a full jury. Those three little words were going to come back to haunt me again and again in the next three years before the action actually came to court. But when I first got the letter I took it in my stride. Everything else was doing brilliantly. I just put it to the back of my mind as a minor glitch. The float of Bank Group was going so well – oversubscribed by ten times – so a solicitor's letter felt unimportant by comparison. So it wasn't enough to bring me down. I was cross about it. I was angry that I had missed out three words in a conversation, but I just thought, fuck it.

For a long time it seemed as if that was the best thing I could have done, because life went on as normal. The next couple of years were just mad with expansion and work and building success on success. The incredible take-off of Fish! in Borough Market turned out to be just the start of it. The figures for Fish! were phenomenal, in terms of the return on capital. But it was a double-edged sword, because it was so outstanding, everybody was just going mad to push the concept for all it was worth. As the chairman of the company, I would be sitting in front of some City financial institution presenting the most incredible expansion opportunities – with Bank making fantastic money, and Fish! even better, and on top of that the projected opening of five or six more branches of Fish!. Investors couldn't believe that we were really getting 150 per cent return on capital. Very often when I used to speak to the City I would actually be playing down how phenomenally successful Fish! was. I would be saying to brokers, 'Look, the rest of the chain isn't going to be like this first one, you know. This is a unique situation and you can't rely on repeating that every time.' Because basically, Fish! was the biggest thing to hit Borough Market since London Bridge fell down! For a long time there had just been a farmers' market three or four times a year, and for the first couple of years after we opened Fish!, we were it. Especially in the summer, when we were able to open up the terrace area, it was a very fashionable venue. We would be serving about 2500 people a week in the summer season, particularly if the weather was good. And each cover had an average spend, before VAT and service, of about £30.

I was finally beginning to relax and enjoy myself a bit at this stage. Over the three years from 1999 to 2001 we ended up opening two more Banks and five more Fish!. The first of the two Bank-style restaurants was Lawn, the one we had bought and re-branded very quickly while we were still waiting to open Fish!. I don't think we put as much heart and soul into it as perhaps we could have. But as far as the City was concerned it was a simple fact that it was an established restaurant which continued to produce some very satisfactory figures. The next Bank we opened was actually in Birmingham, and that was a good experience. I'm a great fan of Birmingham, and I'm always saying that in terms of the eating-out culture it is actually much closer to London than you would think – maybe closer even than some of the other big city centres. You have all those wonderful curry houses in Broad Street, and there's a Hotel du Vin, and of course Raymond Blanc was there as well. So I really enjoyed opening the Birmingham branch of Bank. And we ended up with a Fish! there as well.

The opening rate of the Fish! restaurants was amazing – six altogether in the space of just two years. We had all been waiting to see if Fish! at Borough Market would work, and when it did we went into overdrive. As well as seeing chefs and doing his day-to-day routine, Ronnie Truss was running round the place looking for new sites. The first new site we found was in Battersea on Queen's Town Road. I think it must have brought some mixed emotions to Christian Delteil, because that was where his original Michelin-starred restaurant had been, where he really made his name as a chef in this country. He had a fantastic restaurant there, but he had also been through some hard times there during the recession, so going back to Queen's Town Road was probably quite poignant for him. Still, we all decided to give it a go as the site for the first Fish! branch, and Julian Wickham went in to do the interior. When we opened it was very busy to start with and then levelled off a bit. It was never going to be another Borough Market, and in some ways I wasn't sure whether it was the right site for a Fish!. But with a concept as tailor-made and specific as Fish! the theory was that it could work almost anywhere and we needed to test that. The results were definitely good enough for us to think, 'Right then, where next?'

The next site we chose was in County Hall – on the South Bank of the Thames, where the old Greater London Council used to have its offices and which was now being redeveloped. It was a great location for us, but it turned out to be a difficult site to develop. The build went on for a long time, and we ended up spending a hell of a lot of money on it, over the million pound mark. By this time though, we were actually getting estate agents and property developers phoning us up to offer sites. It had got to the point where having a Fish! coming to your development was a feather in your cap and would encourage other top brands to join in. This was particularly marked at the Mail Box development in Birmingham, which was being done on an old mail sorting office in the canal side area. The directors there were offering us all sorts of enticements to be part of it, including tailor-made units to suit our requirements. It was a measure of what a successful brand Fish! had rapidly become that it was having an impact on multi-million pound developments. That sort of brand recognition is a priceless asset in business. Larger companies spend millions trying to create it, but for us it had come about through following our instincts and gut feelings about what people would respond to. And now it was helping us when it came to expansion. It made Ronnie and me realize that Fish! was literally on the map. We had three restaurants up and running, and now people from all over the country were approaching us, rather than us having to do the running around.

We were contacted by another massive new development that was going on at the time, Canary Wharf in London's old docklands area. So we created a Fish! there as well. But one of my favourite sites of all was in Guildford. It was basically a big glass conservatory perched on top of a car park, looking out over the water across to Guildford Cathedral. It had a terrace that could do 100 people and it was just a fabulous restaurant. When I later bought back part of the group, the Guildford restaurant was one of the ones I bought back – but I had to sell it on to finance the deal. That has always been one of my biggest regrets: that I let that restaurant go. What a lovely site it was. All those initial six Fish! branches we did, from the first at Borough Market, to that great rooftop conservatory in Guildford, were always my favourites. And I still think those six sites were the best ones.

So by the end of 2000 and into 2001, everything was going very well. At this point we had five Fish! locations up and running – Borough Market, Battersea, Canary Wharf, Guildford and Birmingham, with County Hall taking a little longer because of build difficulties. And they were all smashing budgets, everything was very much in control and where we wanted it to be. So I was very comfortable with the way things were going at that point. But there were some underlying issues, and this was when they started to surface. I suppose that is inevitable with a company that is expanding and changing very rapidly. You are so busy fire-fighting and focusing on turning your projections into reality, that the little tensions get ignored. Then when things relax a little, they come to the fore. The first thing we needed to deal with was our positions within the company. Everything had always happened so quickly that there had never been a chance to discuss in detail who would have what title within the company. It was very much a question of someone saying, 'We have to present to the City tomorrow about the flotation, we need to be able to say who the chairman is and so on.' So I ended up as chairman and chief executive, with Ronnie Truss and the others as the executives. Nobody thought much of it at the time, but as we got more and more publicity, and when Entrepreneur of the Year happened, I think some people on the board felt it was becoming too much of the Tony Allan show.

That may have been one of the things weighing with Ronnie, but for him it was probably more the whole situation. I don't think he liked boardroom politics and the element of envy that was creeping in. Ronnie ultimately got a bit fed up with it all and decided he would move on from the company sooner rather than later. There was so much else he was interested in – he was a great sportsman and runner – so I imagine he just thought, why bother. Then early in 2000, while I was away in Barcelona with the family, someone offered him a lot of money for his shares and he sold up and left. He was a very wealthy man who could afford to do his own thing, so he went off and set himself up in sports physiotherapy. I was really disappointed when I got back from Spain to discover that Ronnie had gone with so little warning. He'd been there right from the beginning. He was someone I had met within a very short time of becoming a chef, and he was the mate I turned to when I needed a proper partner for Cutty's. It had been our baby, and now he'd gone off to do something else. Ronnie and I had always made a great team because our skills complemented each other so well, and we always had distinct roles within the partnership. I was the ideas man, the buyer, and the one driven to get up and go to the market in the early hours. Ronnie never had to push me, because that was what I did and he respected that. But what Ronnie was brilliant at was going out and communicating, talking to chefs, selling our company and our brand. I could never have competed with him there. What made it work so well was that our temperaments dove-tailed together so well. I was the extrovert one, taking the lead, doing the publicity – the public face of the company really. I was very driven, and I could be quite hyper. But Ronnie was the calm centre of it all. He was the steady inner core of our business partnership, and it worked very well like that. Good business partnerships are a bit like marriages. If the two people are too much alike, they will clash, and the egos get in the way. But Ronnie and I slotted together to make a great team.

For me, Ronnie going was a turning point. Looking back, I can see that we were probably both feeling pretty much the same way about things. Neither of us were great fans of the City anyway, and without Ronnie's sense of humour, I began to get disillusioned with it as well. For me, being hands on was integral to my sense of achievement and my enjoyment of the work. I've always been motivated by the desire to get really stuck in. But by now we had grown too large for that to be possible in the way it used to be. There were guys that we employed within the various companies that made up our group that I don't think I have ever even spoken to. And there were restaurant managers and chefs that I never had a chance to sit down for a chat with. Before we went public I was completely in tune with everybody down to the guy cutting the fish up and the lad that swept the floor. This is something that entrepreneurs in whatever business say time and again – you do tend to lose touch. But, it's probably unavoidable, because one of the other things you have to bear in mind is that now you have a responsibility to the shareholders, which you didn't have before.

So there are a lot of new demands on you, but something that I should have realized at the time, was that you also have a responsibility to yourself. For one thing you are a shareholder, after all! With BGR, I was actually the majority shareholder. If I had been true to myself and stuck to my personal style a bit more, I think it would have been better for everybody. If I had kept the same mentality and the same work ethic that I had the day before I floated, yes, I would have been looked on as a bit of a maverick, but I probably would still be public today. But having a board and being a plc was a new experience for me and I think, with hindsight, that I let it submerge my identity. I wasn't by any means the only one who went through this. The late 90s were a bit of a weird period for the restaurant industry, as it had become highly fashionable to float restaurants as companies on the market, and this had never happened before. But it was a bull market in those days and it was the trendy thing to do. You only had to pick up the phone to speak to a mate about a fish order to discover yourself being put through to a chef who's suddenly a chief executive! I remember chatting to Mark Hix, of Le Caprice, one of my best friends, and he was a director of a public company.

We had all gone from being very extrovert characters within the catering industry to being directors of public companies. There was a massive list of restaurants and restaurant groups doing it, partly because it was such a successful way of raising money. There was the Chez Gerard group, which is a reliable chain of unpretentious French-style steak and chips restaurants. The Hertford Group didn't have one clear brand but tended to concentrate on American-style diners, with Dakota restaurant as the flagship. Then they launched The Pharmacy as a joint venture with Damien Hurst and Marco. Even the Gaucho Grill went public. To tell the truth, the brokers were so hooked on restaurant ventures you could have got a chip shop away on the market at that time. So all these chefs who would probably have been better off exercising their efforts as genuine restaurateurs were being kept on the straight and narrow by the discipline of being company directors. But that's how it was – it was part and parcel of the success wagon that the whole restaurant industry was on then.

At first I was very upbeat about it all. I thought well, I've had the best part of three years of this and I can get my head down and carry on. But that was beginning to ebb away, and with Ronnie gone, I was beginning to have to acknowledge that I didn't really feel like it any more. The motivation that had got me out of bed at half past two every morning was beginning to dwindle. I was tending to think, I've achieved what I want to achieve from this. I was reaching the point where I didn't believe I would be the person to roll out these restaurants all over the country. I could see a role for myself fronting up the public relations. And I knew my expertise was important when it came to sustaining quality within the restaurants, as well as the culinary side and the economics of menu selection. So I didn't see myself doing what Ronnie had done and pulling out completely. I was quite confident that I could still help the brand. But there was no doubt; I was starting to get itchy feet. Looking back on that whole public company thing, frankly, it was so fucking boring.

It was symptomatic of how I was feeling that I went off and started my own property company in 2000, almost by accident. The stock market went tits up and I thought property would be a better investment, so I started buying houses. What gave me the idea was the difficulty we were having staffing our suburban restaurants. A lot of our staff were immigrants from eastern Europe, and they had nowhere to live. So I was buying cheap housing with them in mind. I started off buying a house for £40,000, which I refurbished and turned into flats. The deal was basically financed by their increased value, because as soon as the property had been revalued I was able to remortgage it. I ended up with about 100 properties on this basis, which were mainly rented to housing trusts for students and asylum seekers.

It was the kind of entrepreneurial project that I enjoy doing – a good idea, a good return, and no need for a lot of long-winded business meetings. I'm very much a concepts person, and I'm very good with individuals, but the restaurant company seemed to have reached a stage where that wasn't the important thing any more. It is a very difficult thing, because up until then my personality being strongly identified with the company was almost our main USP. That seems to happen often where a particular individual has been the driving force behind a brand – I think, for example, Richard Branson hasn't always had very happy experiences with setting up in a plc. I still firmly believe that it goes wrong when you have to get involved with City people, who basically know nothing about your particular business. To me a lot of those City boys are just a bunch of frustrated entrepreneurs themselves. They don't do anything creative themselves; they don't have the actual ideas that are going to generate profit. Instead the biggest decision in their life is whether to say yes or no to someone with a good idea presenting to them to ask for their investment. Ninety per cent of the time they just say no, because that's the safe option and they don't risk showing themselves up. Often I found myself presenting to people who wheeled out the standard accountancy questions, but basically had no idea of what to say to me when it came to specific business issues.

I think that inability to move into the real world of hands-on businesses actually made them very weak in the end. Some of them were almost putty in your hands. And because the City was so cut off from what was going on at the sharp end, there was a great tendency for brokers to be spinning fairy tales about their clients' businesses. Only for us, it wasn't a fucking fairy tale; it was what was actually happening. To them I suppose the presentation that I would walk in with was basically a fairy story with the figures to prove it. And our board seemed to be getting more and more obsessed with the City side of it, rather than the actual business, which was the restaurants. The strangest thing that happened was that the board suddenly decided to change the handling of our press. Instead of dealing with the consumer press, the leisure and lifestyle sections of the newspapers, which is what would actually bring people into restaurants, they suddenly took on a company called College Hill, and changed to doing purely financial PR. I went along with the decision at the time but, thinking back on it now, it was a ludicrous thing for a restaurant company to do. Restaurants are all about buzz, not about financial reports, and sure enough I saw the numbers of bums on seats starting to go down because we weren't being talked about enough.

To an outsider it must have looked a very strange thing to do, but at the time there were a lot of hidden agendas among members of the board. You might have certain non-executive directors who were looking to get some profile for themselves and their other ventures, who wouldn't mind a plug in the financial pages on the back of BGR. I found myself in the ridiculous situation where, as a chef, restaurateur and leading fish expert, the only thing I was talking to the press about was interim results. The only restaurant writer I ever got to talk to was Nick Lander, the food critic of the Financial Times. Everything about the restaurants and what we were trying to achieve went out the window. It was all just results and dividends. You found yourself being run by financial institutions for whom you had no respect. I can remember presenting for a project and thinking to myself, 'Why do I have to share my ideas with these people?' It got to the point in 2000 where I was really questioning why we had bothered to go public at all. So when Ronnie left, I came to the realization that this was not where I wanted to be, and not what I wanted to be doing. I had two or three brilliant concepts up my sleeve, but I just didn't feel as if I wanted to pursue them any further, with things as they were. Normally I have loads of energy and plenty left over to motivate others, but now I felt so cut off from what was going on. I used to go into our Head Office and sit at my desk and feel completely isolated, while everything and everybody went on running around doing whatever it was they were doing. And one day I just thought what the fuck am I doing here?

And all along in the background, the libel action was still going on. It was relentless, week after week, month after month. It was dragging on and on to the point where I can't describe how it was making me feel inside. We had the BGR board meeting every month, and every month I would be asked the question about settling. It was March 1998 when the solicitor's letter had first arrived, and the case eventually came to court in January 2001 – three years later. As time went on it got worse and worse, things seemed to escalate until it was taking over everything. At the beginning it really didn't seem as if it was going to be a big problem. The first Christmas, that would have been '98, I met up with Marco to discuss it man to man. We agreed to settle the dispute and we decided it would be good public relations if we also got together and did something for Great Ormond Street Hospital – put the money to good use, rather than waste it on endless legal fees. And we shook hands on that, but somehow it never happened. Things had got complicated because there were other people involved, all of whom were saying different things all the time. Gordon Ramsay was one of those who was due to be called to give evidence. My lawyer contacted Gordon to see if he would reconsider, and that's when it all started getting really nasty. There were phone calls flying around everywhere with everyone playing the 'he said/you said' game, and the upshot of it all was that I got landed with a charge of perverting the course of justice, as well as the two counts of libel.

By this stage it was becoming a bit of a cause celebre. Marco's lawyer, Keith Schilling, was very well known, and he was in *Hello!* and *Vogue* and all the rest of it. They were getting a lot of publicity – and at the end of the day it is a fact that my legal bills were half of what Marco's were. It meant that Marco was deeply financially committed. He probably would have been quite happy to settle – but his legal fees would have been unsustainable. At that stage I think the betting would have been on Marco maybe winning on one count of libel, but no more than that.

By the end of 2000 it was all getting pretty bad. The court case was scheduled to be held in January 2001 at the Law Courts in the Strand, just at the top of Fleet Street. We were all under a huge amount of stress. Denys was getting worried. Even my mate Vinnie Jones was getting wound up about it – he could see the state Denys and the children were in. So Vinnie invited us all to spend Christmas with him and his wife Tanya in Los Angeles. He was right; it was exactly what we all needed. And we had such a relaxing time. On New Year's Eve we even jetted off to Las Vegas to see James Brown in concert. But then New Year's Day 2001 must have been one of the lowest moments of my life. I remember waking up that morning in the hotel room, and we'd had such a great time the night before, and then it suddenly hit me: this is it. Here we go, it's on us now. I already had a flight booked to take me back to London for rehearsals with my barrister. The court case was only a matter of days away.

Denys came with me to the airport; she would be following on with the children a couple of days later in time to come to court. She said good luck and we parted and I jumped on the plane. And we were both thinking, god, we've had three years of this making our lives a misery. I'm sure to the children he was the big bad wolf of the catering trade. So getting on that flight to go and face it all was a pretty bad feeling. I took some sleeping tablets and managed to sleep pretty much the whole way back to England. I remember landing at Heathrow and the first thing I did was talk to Jeremy Omerod on the phone. It turned out that they had finally managed to trace the woman whose mouth had been stained in Marco's restaurant. She was adamant she didn't want to go to court, but she had agreed to give a statement. It was a boost, because the statement said just what we needed. And I was beginning to think, hell, we're going to win this. I'm definitely going to give it a go.

Then the day came. The press were everywhere. I had actually rented somewhere in London, to be handy for the lawyers and the court. But our home was unliveable in anyway – there were press outside the house, the courts, they were even at the children's school. It wasn't just that it was Marco Pierre White versus Tony Allan; we had the two top libel barristers in the country fighting it out for us. It was like Chelsea versus Arsenal – the London derby of law with George Carmen QC in one corner and Desmond Brown QC in the other. George Carmen even mentions the case in his autobiography. Denys came with me to the court, and for some reason I took my passport and my driving licence with me – I just didn't know what was going to happen, I felt I had to be prepared for anything.

It was one of those bright, clear January mornings – very cold, but very sharp and light, with the sun shining. I remember as I was walking in thinking, what a beautiful day. On a morning like this I should be out pheasant shooting. It's January, the leaves have fallen off the trees and I should be out shooting. Any other time, on a day like this, I would be out with my mates enjoying a lovely day of sport. And then it suddenly came to me – one of those mates would probably be Marco. Because Marco is another keen pheasant shooter and we used to go out a lot together. I thought, this is madness, we should be out together, not fighting in this bloody court. What the fuck are we doing? How did it ever come to this?

I remember it all so vividly. We went into the court room and sat down in the benches, just behind our barrister. Then the jury were sworn in. I remember looking across at Marco, and I was seized with this weird impulse to laugh. His hair was all wild like always and for some reason it struck me that he looked just like Tommy Cooper only without the fez. Yet once upon a time I had a lot of respect for what Marco had achieved. I suppose I still do in some ways, but I really don't want anything to do with him any more, at any level. These days, since that terrible time when we were sitting across from each other in court, I feel that I have moved on so much. Sitting there on the court bench I was thinking what a lot of time I had found for the man over the years, time that really I should have been spending with my wife and my children. I probably had let myself be too close to him, and I needed to distance myself. And somehow, all his glamour seemed to ebb away. I suddenly saw him quite differently. It was a bit like that moment where you meet some glam-rock star from your childhood, and its 30 years later and they are doing a gig in a pub.

And I started laughing to myself and I looked at Denys, and I thought, she has had more than ten years of this guy. So I turned to my barrister and said, 'Can I see you outside?' As soon as we got out into the corridor, I said, 'I will settle.' It had stopped being about me, or even about Marco. I sat in that courtroom and looked at my wife. It was for her that I agreed to settle. In the little side room outside the court I turned round to Desmond Brown and said, 'That's it, I've had enough. I don't want to go on like this. No one's winning, and no one's going to win.'

Denys agreed fully with the decision not to go all the way, despite being an expensive financial decision. But I get pleasure out of it now. I get a sense of satisfaction out of the fact that I could pay and get rid of it. At the end of the day, I did have the funds available and that meant that I got it all out of the way. I was able to settle, all out of my own personal money that I had earned, and I still wasn't reduced back to selling fish out of the back of a van. It was an impact though, financially. I am not a cash-rich person, even though I did have that money in cash at the time. We had to do a few things, like I had to extend the mortgage on our house and stuff like that. But it was well worth it for Denys and the kids. I thought about her and Charlie and Holly and I thought: I'm not going to entertain this man a moment longer. If I had been single, without a loving family, maybe I would have gone on and fought it out to the bitter end, but I realized I had better things to do with my life. So Marco never got his day in court.

And then all hell broke lose with the press. We were running out of the court building onto the Strand, into that bright sunlight, and we were bundled into the back of a car, just like something in the movies. We couldn't get back to the house, the press were camped out. So I told the driver, head straight for the airport, and I got on the mobile to Denys's parents and said, 'Grab the kids and get them to Heathrow, we're catching a plane.'

Chapter Seven

Escape

WE ALL managed to get to Heathrow and we jumped on a plane to LA. As soon as we arrived we made straight for the Four Seasons Hotel. By coincidence that night in Los Angeles it was the Hollywood premiere of *Snatch*, the film Vinnie Jones had been making with Guy Ritchie – a follow-up to *Lock, Stock and Two Smoking Barrels*. Denys and I had grown very close to Vinnie and Tanya, so we surprised them by turning up at the premiere. It was quite a night. I remember we were all in the Four Seasons, and I was wearing this baseball cap with Fish! on it, and it was, as Vinnie's character in *Lock, Stock* said, emotional – even Vinnie had tears in his eyes. Then next day Guy Ritchie went out and got hold of the papers and he was reading out what they were saying. The British journalists were writing that I had settled the court case because I wanted to be able to get away in time to see the premiere of *Snatch*. Vinnie was saying, 'I didn't know you cared' and I was saying, 'no offence, you're a good friend, but not that good!'

Looking back, I haven't regretted flying straight out like that for a second; it was the right thing to do. I had learnt who my true friends were, and it was important to make that statement of going to be with them, rather than dwelling on what had happened. Partly because of our love of pheasant shooting, Marco and Vinnie and I had been in much the same set, and even these days Marco still makes approaches to me and Vinnie to come out. But I don't think I ever would. Maybe some would consider it to be holding a grudge, but I don't see it like that. For me it is more of a case of moving on with my life and going forward, rather than trying to hang on to things that are over and done with. I can't say that the whole business didn't leave a sour taste, though. I was very disillusioned with the restaurant industry after that. And I had parted with around £1.5 million in cash, which anyone would notice. That is a lot of money to go out and earn as an individual. And we'd gone over budget with doing up our new home in north Kent, so life would certainly have been more comfortable if that hadn't happened.

Back at the company, I discovered that all these events had shaken a few things out of the woodwork. At the beginning of it, three years earlier, the board of the plc had been very supportive, mainly because the company had been included in the original action. There was an unstated acknowledgement that the company pretty much revolved round me anyway, and therefore I would have the board's full support. But when push came to shove, it didn't really feel like that. It was decided that I would bear the full weight of costs and pursuing the action as an individual, rather than as part of the company. Regardless of the money, it wasn't a good feeling. I was starting to have had enough. In any case, the personal pressure on me as the company's figurehead continued to be enormous. It got to the point where the share price would plummet if I got up in the morning and farted.

The court case itself hadn't actually caused any of this. What it did was bring out into the open a lot of things that had been going on for quite a while. Although the end of the case brought it all to a head, I think I had actually been feeling this sense of disillusionment for some time. Ronnie Truss had left the company in early 2000, nearly a year before I settled the libel action. I know it must have been a difficult decision for Ronnie. He had about three million shares and the share price, about £4, was phenomenally high for the size of company we were. Ronnie wasn't sure anyway what he wanted to do with the rest of his career, so by the time the shares reached £6, it was just too tempting. When someone came along to buy him out, he moved on. That was a crucial point for me, because Ronnie leaving crystallized all the concerns I had. Eventually I said to the board: 'I think the time is right for me to relax my role.'

You could actually see the colour drain from people's faces. I was sitting there watching them all and I ended up telling them how I really felt. I told them exactly how fed up I was that I hadn't been told about Ronnie's leaving. I know perfectly well I couldn't have stopped Ronnie – they were his shares at the end of the day – but we'd been mates and partners for 14 years. I'm sure Ronnie owes a lot to me in just the same way that I owe a lot to Ron for all that we've achieved together. Hardly any of the current board had been part of our original team. I just looked around at all these guys and thought, what the hell am I doing here? From then onwards I was always telling them at board meetings, 'I think I want to relax my role.' And that made them nervous. I must have been like a broken record to a lot of the directors, always saying, 'I want to stand back.' They would be saying amongst themselves, 'Oh don't worry, he'll be all right tomorrow, massage his ego a bit and he'll be fine.' But they must have been worrying all the time: is he suddenly going to go off and drop us all in it?

I think a lot of people who have been involved in big exciting projects – whether in business or any walk of life – go through this experience. You get a tremendous nostalgia for the early days when you were all up against it. Everybody is working every hour there is and nobody has time for petty personality clashes or self-ishness. It's that early, battling stage of a business that I am best at, but our company was a long way beyond that by the start of the millennium. When we were getting Bank up and running we had had this great idea, and a real close-knit team. We did everything – even the painting and decorating. Those were exciting times, but now I would look around the board, and it felt like we had all become just a bunch of suits. I always kept a soft spot for Michel Roux. He always used to make me think of A.A. Milne's *Winnie the Pooh* books – Michel would definitely have been Owl. He was the wise elder statesman of us. I have so much respect for Michel, but it was quite amusing really. The board knew he was someone whose opinion I valued, so he would be the one that had to do the PR job on me after the board meeting – kind of smooth me down again.

Basically I wasn't getting any support from the board for what I wanted to achieve. Also they wanted to do a lot of things that I really didn't agree with. For example, they were suggesting that we should change all the menus at Fish!, which was not only unnecessary, but also against the whole concept of the brand. My argument was: 'Look, Pizza Express's menu hasn't changed for 30 years, right? And that's part of its selling proposition.' And the Fish! restaurants were still doing very, very well, so for me it was a question of, 'if it ain't broke, don't fix it.' But I was in the position where I was the one having to convince the board of all this. I accept totally that ideas and concepts can get a bit stale, and that's when you have to liven them up a bit – but Fish! in 2000/2001 was anything but stale. It was rocking, it was humming. And I was thinking; this is mine. I made this happen, and everybody was getting rich round me. I felt, I really don't want to listen to all this drivel from the board, why should I?

But getting out of the driving seat was easier said than done. Changing my role was a process that took many months. I call it the 'yeah, but' experience. Every time I would sit down with the stockbrokers and say, 'I basically want to go non-executive, I don't want to be so hands-on any more,' they would say, 'yeah, but this' or 'yeah, but that'. I remember having a meeting with them and I said, 'Look, I've had enough. Tell me exactly what you want me to do. And no "yeah-buts", just a list of what I need to do for you to be OK with it.' So it turned out there were three fundamental things. First of all I had to find a chief executive to take over my position. And it had to be someone with roll-out experience, because we were still in the middle of expanding Fish! into a major chain. Then the next thing was that I mustn't go back to the market for more money. Any money we needed to put the new set-up in place, the company would have to find for itself. The third criteria was that I would find the next few sites to develop for the new branches of Fish!. It was like being in some kind of fairy story – I had these three tasks to complete and then the spell would be lifted.

I found a guy called Paul Gilligan, who had been with Pizza Express and had plenty of experience with property, to take on my role. Not quite as chief executive, but more as a chief operating officer. Then there was the second requirement, to finance the next stage of the company's development – the plan to roll out lots more branches of Fish! throughout the South East. To do that we sold off the original Bank restaurant, and its spin-off, Bank Westminster, but we came up about half a million short of what we needed, so I put that in personally. Of all the business decisions I have made, selling Bank is probably the one I regret the most. I was proud of that restaurant and what we achieved with it – and it represented happy times for me. But I knew I couldn't stand still, I had to move on, and to do that we had to have funds for the next phase. Finding the sites for the new Fish! branches was almost the easiest part of it, because we already had several in the pipeline. And that was when Fish! became a separate company in its own right. I agreed to stay on as chairman, but it would be a salaried position, with the agreement that I wasn't going to get involved in the day-to-day operations. By this stage I just wanted it all sorted out, and Paul Gilligan, the new man in charge, was very confident about the concept of Fish!. He even felt we didn't have to confine ourselves to the M25 area – he was talking about Leeds for example. By now we were opening new branches for fun; we were doing it so fast! I had been involved personally in the first six, and I think the last one I had much to do with was the one on King's Road, which must have been the eighth. After that I was a bit remote from it all.

It became an odd time for me. I felt in some ways as though I was in limbo – not hands-on with the restaurants any more, but not starting any new projects either. It was quite hard getting up in the mornings without those old motivations to energize you. And I remembered a little while before, getting a call from the broker at our new firm of brokers, and he had been suggesting that the company was depending too heavily on my name and my personal identity. I think he had actually said something like, 'This isn't Tony Allan plc.' He was saying, 'You are the chairman of a plc, you shouldn't still be so hands-on, getting up to buy fish at 2.30 every morning.' We were capitalized at around £70 or £80 million and basically his message was I needed to show a bit of respect for my status. And finally, by the middle of 2000, with Fish! starting to roll-out across the country, I took him at his word. I thought – I'm going to start relaxing now. Sometimes I'd go missing from the office for as long as two or three weeks at a stretch, unless someone phoned to say they needed a signature. Basically

I had put a sign on my office door saying: 'Gone Fishing' – except in my case, I had gone shooting.

It was a friend, Brian Bourne, who had first got me interested in shooting clay pigeons on holiday. I enjoyed it and found it quite natural, but the moment I got really hooked was during our millennium holiday in Barbados. That was when I first got to know Vinnie Jones properly. I had been sea fishing and caught a lovely big fish which I brought back to the hotel and commandeered the kitchen so I could cook it myself, and invited Vinnie and his family to share it with us. Then we started shooting a few clays together while we were in Barbados. Vinnie is the son of a gamekeeper, and he's a great countryman with a wonderful knowledge and love of wildlife. Someone had told him I was a keen birdwatcher, so Vinnie was testing me out a bit to see whether I was all talk or not. He said, 'So what's the other name by which a hedge sparrow is known in the countryside?' I certainly didn't have to think about that one, I just said, 'It's a dunnock.' I passed my initiation test, and I was a member of Vinnie's gang – mind you there were only the two of us in it! But Vinnie and Brian got me interested in pheasant shooting, along with John Ward the gunsmith, who was also a friend of Vinnie's.

When I got back to England they invited me shooting with them. The shoot was at Shadwell, a big estate owned by the Dubai royal family. We all met up in a nice country hotel at Newmarket the night before and had a great evening, and then we were up early the next morning a bit worse for wear, to go off shooting. It was the most fantastic day. I was standing there in front of the wood, and I could hear noises and breaking branches in the trees as a team of beaters walked through it towards me. Then the first partridges and pheasants came flying out. It was so exciting. Luckily for me the first birds didn't come anywhere near me, because I don't think I would have known what to do. But I soon got the hang of it and had the most brilliant time. Then we stopped for a break and a bit of picnic lunch, and there we were in January in the English countryside eating sausages and mash and drinking the most beautiful Chateau Petrus. I was totally hooked, but it was right at the end of the shooting season, so I would have to wait until next autumn until I could try it again.

But I was busy in the meantime. I went to John Ward's shop and got myself set up with some shooting lessons. He recommended George Digweed, one of the best shots in the country, and I spent practically the whole summer with him having lessons using clay pigeons. Then I went back to John Ward and said, 'I'd better get the clobber, too,' because shooting is a very traditional and old-fashioned sport. Everybody gets dressed up in tweed shooting suits which have hardly changed since Edwardian times, with specially made breeches and jackets and long woollen socks in fancy colours. I got myself 12 shooting outfits made and I was ready for the season to begin. That season and the one after, I must have gone out shooting more than 200 times. My shooting was like my business career – I packed as much shooting into the space of a couple of years as a country gentleman might do in ten. I went all over the country to shoot. There are some famous shoots on Exmoor and I tried those. I went up to Wales, to Cumbria – to Scotland even. And closer to home, there are some lovely shoots on the South Downs which I enjoy.

These days I don't do quite as much shooting as I did in those first couple of seasons when I was discovering it for the first time, but I still try to get out at least once a week through the season – sometimes more. Vinnie and I shoot a lot together, and there is always an element of competition between us, which adds a bit of spice to the day. The shooting bug bit me right from day one. I loved the traditional element of it – all that dressing up in loud check tweeds, wearing socks and fancy garters and all that. And the craic is very important to a shooting day; the social side of it is just as big a part of it all as the sporting element. As I have done more shooting, I've got used to all the old-fashioned element of it, but it blew me away to begin with. These days the social and the sporting are the two elements that I really value. When I am shooting with a bunch of mates, we can have a bit of a laugh, and get away from it all. But the other element, the personal desire to shoot well and to learn about how the sport works, is becoming a really important part of it for me. Lots of people are against sports like shooting, but you will find quite a lot of chefs who either shoot or fish. I think it is because we are very much in touch with where food comes from. Unlike people who buy their meat ready-packed in a supermarket or in a burger bun from McDonald's, we do actually know right from the beginning about the food chain. So it's not that big a step for us to go out and get the meat ourselves, rather than buying it from the butcher.

Right from the start I have found shooting to be a marvellous way of relaxing. It is challenging and stimulating, but totally removed from work. Through shooting, I have met true and decent people in all sorts of walks of life who have become really good friends. The best friends I have are through meeting people connected with the sport. During the period leading up to, and after, the court case, I was very disillusioned with what had been going on, and shooting was the best escape I could have found. I'm sure it helped me get through some of the rough patches. At the end of the day, when you have an experience like that with a hobby, and you can afford to do it, why would you want to go back to work and face lawyers and brokers? I was increasingly coming to believe that the people I dealt with in the city were just frustrated types. Unsurprisingly, I wanted to spend more time with my real friends out in the country.

For the first two or three months after the court case, that was exactly what I did. I kept myself to myself and concentrated on the things that interested me. One of the things I did was start building up my personal property portfolio again. I went down to the Medway and started buying some houses for flat conversions, which was all very successful. Those kinds of projects do tend to come instinctively to me. And it was a good thing to do at the time, because I had lost a bit of confidence, and I needed to reassure myself that I'd still got it. By the middle of 2001 it seemed as if a lot of chapters in my life were coming to a close. The court case was over. I had pretty much sung my swan song for the company. I had found them the £9 million in cash they needed to expand Fish!. Paul Gilligan was in place, and there were a number of restaurant sites on stream. I had agreed to stay on as chairman of Fish!, but I knew that it was time for someone else to come in and take the brand forward.

The next project that came along turned out to be something I would never have expected. I was asked to do a cookery photo shoot for *FHM*, the men's magazine. The story was all about weird-looking fish, and some varieties of fish can look pretty strange! The idea was that I would get hold of all these odd varieties for the magazine and they would photograph them and I would do a few recipes for the fish. So I phoned Giorgio Locatelli, an Italian chef based in London, who is a good friend of mine, and asked him if he wanted to come and play around with these fish with me. He agreed to come along, and when I mentioned this to my PR girl she thought it sounded like something the BBC might possibly be interested in, so she invited a friend of hers from the Beeb to come along and watch the shoot. Of course, Giorgio and I were just messing around having a laugh throughout the shoot, but they loved it, and the next thing we heard was that they wanted to do a pilot show for a possible BBC series. In the autumn of 2001 we got called into the White City to the BBC studios and had meetings with BBC2 and the Food and Drink department and they decided to commission a whole series, to be called Tony and Giorgio, which was great.

But the big thing that happened for everybody just about then was 9/11. September 11th, 2001 came along and it was: welcome to the real world. It immediately made life very difficult for everybody in the hotel and restaurant trade. Paul Gilligan, who had taken over from me, was in the middle of rolling out the expansion of Fish!. They opened seven new restaurants in the six weeks after September 11th, but it was a disastrous time to be opening new restaurants. I was warning the board about how business would suffer in this situation. I wanted to sell some of my shares and become completely non-exec. But the board had heard all about the new TV series. Their thinking was that the company shouldn't lose me, just as I was doing a prime time BBC television series, so they still wanted my name connected with the company. The stock market was in a mess as well, so it wouldn't have been a good time to sell shares anyway, so I agreed to go along with it, and we all just got our heads down and got on with things.

For me, that meant concentrating on the television series. We started filming properly at the beginning of 2002, and right from the start Giorgio and I had such a great laugh. And it was another adventure. I had started out as a chef in the great hotel kitchens. Then I became a wheeler-dealing fishmonger. Then Bank had turned me into a celebrity restaurateur, and finally I had become the chairman of a plc. Now I was going to be a television chef – what an amazing roller-coaster.

It was quite an eye opener to be working with the BBC. We were filming most of the series in the kitchen of my home in north Kent and when the crew started coming into the house you have this huge team of people descend on you. There were three cameramen, a director, an assistant director, the producer, the assistant producer and by the time you include people like the girls from the Home Economics department it added up to about 24 people – and at least 30 days of the filming was in the house. And for the first couple of days it was quite tricky, because it just wasn't working. What would happen is that Giorgio and I would be larking around like two kids during the rehearsal and one of us would make a joke and everybody would be cracking up. Then the director would say, 'Great, let's get that, do it again.' And of course we couldn't, it wasn't spontaneous any more. So in the end one of the directors, Dan, said, 'I think we'll achieve a lot more by just filming this real time and then editing it down afterwards. We'll film these two guys cooking and out on location and then we can do the technical side back in the studio and edit it in later as cutaway shots.'

So we hit on that formula and it worked straight away. Everything was quick, the banter was fast, and the whole thing was much sharper. And of course we got some of the unpredictable things into it. I remember the way the hangover food episode came about was very funny. We were filming and I took Giorgio out for a bit of a drink up and it goes to his head quite easily. So there we were, Giorgio was pissed and we were in the back of a taxi – filming

– and his wife rings up wanting to know where the hell he is. Then six o'clock the following morning they wanted to film us coming down the stairs hungover. That didn't take much acting – especially for Giorgio, he had a stinker! Then we had me taking him round the corner to the caff for a fry-up and Giorgio cooking the Italian version of hangover food, which is just the same as normal Italian food – pasta.

We ended up in some hilarious situations. A publishing company, Fourth Estate, was trying to persuade us to do a book of the series and since both Giorgio and I are big football fans, they took us up to Leeds to see England play Italy at Elland Road. Obviously with Giorgio being Italian, I was taking the mickey when England went one–nil up, but I was laughing on the other side of my face by the time Italy had scored twice and won 2–1. Then what we suddenly realized was that we now had to get out of the ground. There was no mistaking that Giorgio was Italian – particularly since he was cheering and shouting in Italian – and I'd just got back from Portugal with a real Mediterranean tan. I was trying to get Giorgio to shut up, and we just ran and jumped straight in the first car with a familiar face behind the wheel. It was this tiny little Renault Clio and happened to be driven by a guy from Waterstones that we'd met with the publishers. I think he was a bit surprised when these two guys suddenly jumped in, but I was saying, 'Please, you've got to get us to our hotel because this guy's Italian and he's going get me murdered if he keeps on chanting the score (which Giorgio was doing at the time).' I think by then there were seven of us crammed into the Clio, but we made it back to the hotel. It turned out that it was the England team's hotel, and by the time we got back there, the bus was just dropping them all off – Beckham, Sven-Goran Eriksson, and the rest, all licking their wounds!

Giorgio had this problem; it used to make me laugh. Anything to do with food, he just couldn't restrain himself. We would be sitting there at the breakfast bar in the kitchen and Denys would come in with the weekly shopping. To start with Giorgio is a total gentleman, so the moment he sees my wife carrying bags of shopping he rushes to help – but then he couldn't keep his hands off it. He would grab the bags, plonk them on the breakfast bar, and he would start going through them, sorting out all the foodstuffs. And this was a family shop; so of course, there would be all sorts of TV dinners, ready-made toad-in-the-hole for the kids and everything. Giorgio would get hold of the toad-in-the-hole and hold it up and just look at it and raise his eyebrows and give this sarcastic shrug of the shoulders as if to say: 'And you call yourself a chef!' But Giorgio is like a puppy around food – he just loves it and can't stop himself from cooking. In the end I used to have to say to him: 'Giorgio, you can't be here in the kitchen cooking everything for everyone the minute you walk in because we'll never get any work done.'

Another funny moment came up when we were doing the deal for the book of the series. We were invited along to Fourth Estate's offices at the bottom of the Fulham Road. It was on a Friday evening, and it was really a bit of a pain. The parking round there is terrible, and I didn't want to be up in town on a Friday night. And Giorgio was very busy because he'd just left the Zeferano restaurant to go and set up on his own, and he was doing a lot of consulting as well. But anyway, I turned up in my Ferrari, and Giorgio pulls up in his leathers on his Ducati motorbike, and we walked into the foyer together. They had one of these functions boards like a hotel, and I remember it had the launch party for Pamela Stephenson's book on Billy Connolly, and also: 'Chefs Tony Allan and Giorgio Locatelli sign contract for a new book.' That didn't go down very well with us at all. We'd been dragged here on a Friday night when we had better places to be and we certainly weren't planning on signing anything. So we marched into this room with faces like thunder and they're busy opening the champagne, and we're going to be spoiling their party. And then the publisher mentioned what the advance payment was, and without a word we reached for the champagne. I think the total advance was in excess of £750,000. That included payments for the BBC rights and agent's fees and so on, but Giorgio and I certainly got half a million between us – so yes, the functions board was right, Tony Allan and Giorgio Locatelli were signing a contract that evening!

It was a busy period for me, with filming for the TV series and doing the book, though during the summer months I didn't have the pheasant shooting to tempt me away from work. I had been at the house filming one day when I got a phone call from the office, saying could I come to an emergency board meeting. Jeremy Omerod was leaving as finance director and they were getting someone new in. So I went along. That was when I discovered that this mountain of cash we had when I last looked had somehow turned into a serious debt problem. The board had paid Jeremy off and replaced him, as well as bringing in some new non-exec directors. I remember going back into the office and sitting down at this board meeting with basically a bunch of strangers. I looked round and all the familiar faces – Ronnie, Jeremy, Christian and all the rest from the old days – had all gone. Paul Gilligan was there of course, but I had only known him a short time, and that really just left Michel Roux. There were two or three people I didn't know who were talking about finance. Of course I knew exactly what they were saying about the fiscal side of things, but what struck me was that they had no real feel for the company. I didn't get the sense that they had any real knowledge of what had made us successful in the first place – and here we were, completely in the shit.

It was easy to see what had gone wrong. It was a combination of two circumstances that added up to really bad timing. Arguably, I think the company was over-expanding – it was certainly expanding too rapidly. And it was doing that within the context of September 11th which was a global event that had the capacity to scupper any expansion from even the biggest companies for several months to come. A lot of people have been accused of hiding behind September 11th, but with something like the restaurant business, it really did have an impact – it completely crushed Fish!. And it wasn't just us either, you could see it through the fishmongery side of the business. The orders for fish coming in from our regular clients were smaller, and it wasn't because they were using other suppliers, it was because they were having a bad time too. I looked at the figures for our restaurants, especially the more recently opened ones, and the writing was on the wall. Even without 9/11 I don't think we could have sustained the rate of new openings that Paul was rolling out. Maybe it's OK opening 13 or 14 restaurants in a very short space of time, but you have to be able to give each one the same degree of individual attention that we had lavished on the first six.

When journalists asked me about it at the time, I was the first to admit that the later Fish! branches probably hadn't had the same TLC that we used to give them. You couldn't get away from the fact that, with the exception of Surbiton, it was the restaurants opened under Paul's direction that had to be closed first. But I didn't feel angry about it, because a roll-out is a roll-out, and that was the company's plan, and what Paul had been appointed to do – so there was no point in 'jobbing backwards' as the stockbrokers say. There were a couple of things that were not great business practice, things I would certainly have handled differently myself. This was especially in the area of our cash reserves, which could have been used more wisely – instead of which there had been a tendency to throw money at problems. Basically, though, we just had to get on with seeing what could be done to fix it. And according to the board, that was where I came in. But I had very mixed feelings. It was such a disappointment, after all we'd done in the past, to look at the cover numbers in the restaurants and know in my heart of hearts that the takings were simply not enough to sustain a sufficient return on the capital invested in opening them. Chefs had been moved around, and the feedback I was getting from the staff on the ground, in the restaurants, was bad. The original Fish! in Borough Market was the one bright spot, it was still doing phenomenal trade.

I listened to everything the board was saying. They were talking about the potential for the TV series when that came out – that it could be a lifeline. They had an idea that television exposure would kick start business again, and that I would step in and recreate the same buzz there had been with the original restaurant openings. I think their vision was of me being a kind of flying trouble-shooter going from restaurant to restaurant sorting everything out. The basic game plan, as I understood it, was that we would pare back down to our core business. The board wanted to try to keep ten restaurants open, while Paul would go round trying to sell the others off, most of which were already closed anyway. They were keen to keep me on board, especially with the television link, and they were offering me £150,000 a year to stay on. We also had a team of company doctors from Postern in to do the whole cost-cutting, income-maximizing routine. So I agreed to stick with it initially, and we went along to see the brokers and outline this game plan in the late spring of 2002. But within weeks you could tell it wasn't going to work. Every day there was a catalogue of disasters. Again it was just things that I regard as really basic business practice – like using your full month's credit with contractors – that were being handled really naively. By June we were having emergency meetings practically every single morning to ask ourselves: are we still solvent?

Then I got a call at home asking me would I come in to attend a meeting with the bank in order to support the plan being put forward by the board and Postern. By this time I was very dubious about the whole thing. I had been at arm's length from the company for no more than 18 months, two years at a maximum, and I knew full well what had happened in that time. I remember asking them exactly what they thought my role would be. I had the phone on loudspeaker, and I was standing by the breakfast bar listening. It was about eleven o'clock at night; the whole thing was quite a bizarre conversation. They began by saying things like 'It's your concept' and 'We need you to go round the ten remaining restaurants on a consultancy basis.' But then gradually it started to become an ultimatum. It was turning into 'You are going to do this' and 'You will do that ...'. I wasn't too thrilled about that, and then I started to feel as though they were calling me into question as well. Someone started talking about a loan account I was meant to have through the company, and how the company had been very good to me over the Marco Pierre White case. The general gist was 'You know the company supported you through your problems with Marco Pierre White.' They were probably talking about the way the accounting had been done, where I think I had originally used a company account before paying in my own private money to settle the case. But they were trying to use it in a way I didn't like. They were going on about everything, trying to bully me, so I just said: 'I think you guys are misinformed.'

That call was the end as far as I was concerned. I just said, 'No I'm not doing it.' I felt as if I was in the army and had disobeyed an order. They said, 'What do you mean you're not doing it?' I said, 'Exactly that, I'm not doing it.' They were furious. They said, 'So you're going to see this go into administration?' and then one of them said to me, 'and you'll probably be one of the people trying to buy it back won't you?' At that point I hadn't really thought about that, but the way they were ranting on, I thought to myself well, you never know, maybe. But all I said was no. So I was made redundant, and that was it. The next thing was that the board applied for a court order and Fish!, my baby that had done so well, was put into administration.

Chapter Eight

A Fishing Trip

W E DID all get together – myself, the board, Postern and the bank – and make one last effort to pull things out of the fire, but the meeting didn't go particularly well. Basically the conversation was as follows. Bank managers: 'Will you put some more money into the company?' Me: 'No.' Them: 'Why not?' Me: 'For starters, I haven't got that kind of money, and even if I did have it, I don't think that's how I would invest it.' Them: 'Do you know how much money the bank stands to lose?' Me: 'Do you know how much money I've already lost? Because for every million you've lost I've lost three times as much, right.' And that was it after that. Postern said they would go ahead and seek the order to go into administration and I was made redundant from my position as executive chairman.

At that stage I still owned over 30 per cent of the company. Ronnie Truss had been out completely since 2000, and when Jeremy Omerod left he had sold a lot of his shares, though I think he still had a fair few left. My brother Mark had already sold more or less all of his. So I had the most shares of anybody, even the institutions. It's quite hard though, to evaluate exactly how much I lost, because the value of the shares had been steadily declining for some time. In some ways I had already subconsciously written off my equity in the company in terms of wealth. By the time we had had to issue an emergency profits warning, the shares were tumbling. In the end I think they were down to about ten pence from three pounds. But at one stage the whole thing had been worth an awful lot of money. There was a point where I had 54% of the company and the shares were up to about £4.20, and I was featuring quite strongly on the Sunday Times Rich List.

After September 11th you could tell that it was going to be important to spread your assets a bit more, and at this time I was getting interested in my property plans, so a lot of my money was diverted there. By the time the company was really on the slide, it no longer represented the bulk of my capital, even though I still retained my 30 per cent holding in the company. But it was still a lot of shares, and it was awful watching them dwindle away and not being able to do anything about it. Whichever way you do the accounting, more or less overnight I had lost about £15 million – and that's a conservative estimate. It depends what you take to be the share price. The shares had recently been trading at around £3, and I think I had something like five million shares still in the company. But earlier in the year they had been at between £4 and £4.20 – though even that was lower than they had been. The market as a whole went down after 9/11, but by summer 2002, the restaurant industry was beginning to get back on its feet, it was a recovery period. Maybe if Fish! had tightened its belt more successfully, things could have improved. Perhaps Paul Gilligan, who had taken over my role, could have taken a more hard-nosed approach with the contractors who were still working on various restaurants and got them straight off site, rather than continuing until the end of the contract.

I suppose ideally I should have walked in, sacked everybody, got Christian Delteil back over from Bank and run it all myself. I would have kept the main restaurants open and then expanded gradually and selectively. With hindsight, I think part of the trouble was that Paul was in above his head. He knew commercial property better than the restaurant business, and all his expansion work with Pizza Express had been during a bull market, where everybody was making money. I think the test of an entrepreneur, or any businessman, is if you can still manage comfortably during a recession. And maybe I gave Paul too much responsibility, but I have always given my staff their head, and it has always worked for me. I also stick by my choice of Paul Gilligan for the job. He was on the main board of Pizza Express and had opened 30 restaurants for them. Frankly he was a far more suitable man to roll out Fish! than I was. I'm great working on goals, and I really enjoy creating concepts and making them work, but there were a few people in the organization at the time who would have agreed with me that I was probably not the person to roll Fish! out. In that case, should I have sold my shares and left the company completely, rather than end up with the responsibility for a mess that wasn't of my making? That was never going to happen. Regardless of commercial sense, I would never have severed my ties with the company. I loved Cutty's. I had started it from a 400 quid loan and an old van all those years ago. And Fish! was the same, particularly that first one in Borough Market which had been the beginning of so many amazing times for me. From the day of flotation, the guys that I worked with – the team that built Bank and Cutty's and everything else – were gradually engulfed by the City. Almost without noticing, we had lost track of the need to look after the customer by providing a quality product with competitive pricing, and we had ended up chasing some abstract set of numbers pulled out of thin air by someone sitting at his desk in the Square Mile. And I had gone along with it.

The administrators were pretty efficient, keeping as many restaurants running as possible in order to try and get some kind of cash flow and protect their value as going concerns. Then it was just a matter of getting the creditors paid off in order of priority – and that was when I felt quite hurt that some of the non-executive directors didn't show much loyalty to the company. Compared with the passion I had felt for what we were doing, it made me think perhaps I should just have cut and run when the share price was at its highest. But ironically it turned out well for me, because sticking with it eventually gave me the opportunity to do one of the best deals I have ever done – which was to buy the company back from the administrators.

The germ of the idea that it might be possible had been planted in my mind during that phone conversation, where the guys were taunting me that I would buy it back. Thinking about that conversation I eventually got in touch with a guy I'd met way back in Christmas 1997. He was a businessman called Andrew Cohen who had been one of the first subscribers to the original Bank group flotation. Not only was Andrew one of the original investors, but he was also one of the guys that never sold his shares, so I knew he still had a belief in what I was trying to do. I had always found him to be a very straightforward bloke and easy to talk to. So I rang him and asked, 'How would you feel about the possibility of coming in with me and trying to buy it back?' He certainly didn't say no immediately, so I went over to the City and had a meeting with him and we chatted about how we might go about it. Andrew's expertise was great to have when it came to negotiating with the administrator.

One of the main issues was that Borough Market Fish!, which was a key site, was so valuable as a restaurant site in its own right. So there were a lot of people within the industry who would be keen to get their hands on it. Several of the other London sites were also very attractive to restaurateurs, which meant there was still quite a bit of viability left in the company. Then I started hearing that the administrators were getting a lot of interest in the company. I gather Pizza Express had a look, and Conran, and the Loch Fyne group. So there were a lot of people who might be in the bidding, whether for the group as a whole, including the fishmonger's business, or just for particular restaurant sites. I knew I could be in with a shout as well, but I needed someone to help me with it, and it was Andrew who agreed to step in and set up the deal.

He contacted the administrators and we put in our bid. It got to the point where we were down to the last two or three of us still in the bidding, and we were really pushing hard. Fortunately we had a good case to make. I had a proven track record. Also we could offer continuity, which is very important when you still have a couple of hundred staff on the payroll wondering what their future will be. Andrew and I knew we could get things up and running again quickly, and with a minimum of hassle. I'm sure this was something the administrators were taking into account, but then we had a sudden setback. It was a very unexpected blow for me, and made doubly worse by the fact that it was my own brother, Mark, who suddenly jumped into the bidding against me. Mark had formed a team including some of those who had been directors of the original Cutty's and one of the company doctors from Postern. They made a direct approach to the administrators to break up the business, so that they could buy just the fishmongery side of it, which was Cutty's the wholesaler and Jarvis, the retail outlet in Kingston-upon-Thames. This went totally against the understanding I had with Mark that if I managed to buy the company back he would become the director in charge of the fishmongery side – which was pretty much what he had been doing all along.

I'll never forget the first time I discovered what he was doing. I was having a brief family holiday in Sardinia and the local shop had a copy of *The Times*, and there it was on the front page of the business section: 'Allan gets battered by brother'. Apparently Mark's offer had been accepted by the administrators before I'd even been told that he'd made a bid. What a way to find out about it. I just couldn't believe what he'd done. My mind went racing back to those days in the 80s when I had got Cutty's going, and my brother had come out of college and I was able to offer him a job. And now he was buying it out from under me. So I got on the phone to him there and then from Sardinia. He was quite pleased with himself I think, and in the end I thought, what's the point, and just said, 'Congratulations, then'. I didn't bother to keep the sarcasm out of my voice either. Because what frustrated me was that it was such a stupid thing to do in any case – regardless of us being brothers. Cutty's and Fish! were very dependent on each other. That had been one of core elements of the strategy of the original company, to have supply-side and demand so well integrated. During the post-9/11 slowdown, Cutty's other wholesale business had dwindled slightly, so by this point, Fish! represented more than 30 per cent of its turnover. It was foolhardy to buy Cutty's separately and just hope that whoever got Fish! would continue to use an independent Cutty's as its supplier. Did my brother naively assume that he would have a ready-made client base? Or perhaps he took it for granted that despite what he had done, I would forgive and forget if I did succeed in buying back Fish!?

Vinnie and his family had come out to join us in Sardinia, and I was still waiting to hear from Andrew Cohen about what we could salvage from the deal. It was at the beginning of August, less than a fortnight after my abortive phone call with my brother, that I got another call – and this time it was good news from Andrew. He said, 'We've got it back.' The administrators had agreed to sell us the seven branches of Fish! that we wanted (basically the ones I had originally opened) plus our head office in Air Street, and – crucially – the retail fish outlet, Jarvis. I remember turning up at our head office at 9.30 on the Tuesday morning to meet Andrew and sign the papers. I was thinking how worried my brother must be about whether the new owners of Fish!, whoever they might be, would continue to use Cutty's. If they didn't, basically he wouldn't have a business. I remembered how arrogant he'd been on the phone before, and I couldn't help myself. So I picked up the phone and got through to Mark. He said, 'What do you want?' I said, 'I'm just informing you that as the successful bidder for Fish!, I'm now your biggest customer.' There was just a silence, and then I said, 'Oh, and by the way, I'm also your second biggest customer. I bought Jarvis as well.' The line went dead.

But having the last laugh isn't much good when it's your own family, so when Mark's business partner called back, I offered to meet up with them all so we could talk through how the new arrangements would work. I explained that I wanted to build up the reputation of Jarvis's retail business and that would mean taking on a lot of buying personally. I was planning to start going back into Billingsgate and also to rebuild my connections with the coastal suppliers. That still left plenty of opportunity for Mark though, and I said, 'Let's keep the position where Cutty's supplies the seven Fish! restaurants, and you have a chance to build that right up again, as long as you can keep the standard the same as Cutty's was at its best.' Today I still stand by that as being a fair deal for all of us.

Then it was time for Andrew Cohen and me to start going round the restaurants to see exactly what we had just bought ourselves. We toured round, eating lunch and dinner in all the different branches, inspecting the fridges, watching the staff at work. I was checking the quality of the fish and how it had been cut and prepared for us. Unfortunately it was a complete eye opener. It took me right back to the bad old days at Salter's Court – poor quality fish which had been carelessly handled. It was the very thing that had originally spurred me to set up Cutty's, and make it the best there was, and now it had come full circle. So I was very down about it. I had a conversation with my brother, and I couldn't help showing how upset I was. I was saying, 'This is ridiculous, regardless of whether it's me or not, it's a fish order worth £15,000 or £20,000 a week to you, and you're risking losing it by not supplying a decent product. Look, the quality of the product of Cutty's is the very thing that got us where we are today, and you're just trashing it.'

It was true. Cutty's was what had launched my whole career – and it had made my brother a millionaire as well because I had given him three million shares in the business. I think us being brothers actually made things more difficult than if we had been strangers. If it had just been a man-to-man business deal I would have said: 'Your product is crap, I'm taking my business elsewhere.' But as brothers we had so much history between us. It took me right back to when we were kids and the whole family had to tiptoe round Mark because of his exams and his football and everything. Everybody was always just making plans for Mark and his starry future, and that was an excuse for everything. And I suppose on his side, Mark would have been thinking, here's his kid brother who has outshone him, and now he's trying to pull rank again. Mark was also furious – and probably frightened – because he'd stretched himself to buy Cutty's on the assumption that it would keep the regular business from Fish!, and now that didn't look like it was going to happen. If only we could have talked to each other without all that going on, I could have said, 'Look, neither of us wants you to lose this business, let's just sit down together and work out what can be done.' But two brothers, born within two years of each other? That was always going to get in the way, and in the end it did.

I needed a supplier I could trust, that I could phone up knowing I could do a deal and build a good relationship. By the autumn it had become obvious that the only person who could do that was actually me! So there I was again, after all these years, getting out and buying a van and going back to the fishmarkets again. Obviously the loss of the Fish! business was a big blow to Cutty's, which by now had another name, because I had always retained the rights to the actual 'Cutty's' brand. My brother renamed it Direct Seafood and when he lost the Fish! order he merged with a well-known West End butchers and they ended up supplying mass catering for rail operators and airlines. It is a sad thing to see a business that was once the blue ribbon of fishmongery end up supplying the most notoriously inedible food there is – the old 'British Rail sandwich', and the economy class foil tray – but at least I still have the name.

At the time I was far too busy to dwell on what was happening with the old fishmongers business, because I was heading into a difficult period for the reborn Fish!. But it was so exciting, all my energy came right back. First of all I needed to get the figures right. Basically the deal had cost Andrew and me about two million, which bought seven restaurants, including the original Borough Market Fish!, the head office, and Jarvis the fish retailer. I worked out that since Borough Market was still doing very well, I could quite quickly get it to the point where it would be making a million a year again. With the other six restaurants that weren't doing so well, I reckoned that at worst we could pull in £100,000 a year from each of them – which wasn't so very different from the original projections. I thought Jarvis, the fish store, was probably good for a further hundred thousand. So that was a potential line of one and three-quarter million pounds before the head office costs. It already had the makings of a good balance sheet, and then we got approaches from individuals interested in one or other of the restaurant sites. That meant that we were able to sell off the restaurants in Birmingham, Guildford and Canary Wharf fairly rapidly, which brought in around £700,000. In the end the net position was that we had got the company back for just over a million quid. It was a fabulous deal.

But there was still a hell of a lot of work to do for me and Andrew. One of the things giving me confidence was that Andrew Cohen is a very straight down the line businessman. He's not a restaurateur; he's someone who invests in people. So in his view, it wasn't really a case of buying a bunch of restaurants, it was me and my vision that he was actually backing. Andrew doesn't go much for the showbiz side of the restaurant industry either, he's not a great believer in PR, and working with him was to prove a good discipline for me. Our starting point was that we were a small restaurant company sitting on a lot of capital, and we had to make that work really hard so that we would get good returns over the next three years. The next question was how to make that happen. Andrew was convinced that Fish! as a national brand was a concept that didn't work. Obviously, with my passion for the idea, it was tempting to give him an argument on that. But after all, the proof of the pudding is in the eating, and Andrew could always point to the hard fact that rolling out Fish! hadn't worked the first time, so why would it this time? I would have been making excuses about why some of the branches hadn't worked. You could point to inexperienced teams being put in. Also, by that stage there was very little direction. It needed a really strong figurehead to push the vision into reality. I couldn't disagree that the last 12 or 15 openings had been a bit rudderless.

There was also a very good reason, which we both agreed on, for not revisiting the original Fish! concept. We were now at the end of 2002, whereas Fish! had started back in the late 90s, and there had been a hell of a change in public taste since the millennium. Fashions change very quickly in the restaurant industry, and the whole design and feel of trendy restaurants had changed. As we travelled round the restaurants, it became more and more obvious that we couldn't just do a rerun of Fish!. The place to start had to be our flagship, the Borough Market restaurant. As far as the public was concerned, the Fish! brand had more or less disappeared off the map. Despite this, Fish! Borough Market was still doing well in its own right as a fish restaurant. So it had the potential to re-establish us and get our name back out there. We decided to keep it as Fish!, but to give the restaurant a major refurbishment. Luckily for us the relaunch of Borough Market Fish! coincided with the screening of the BBC television series Giorgio Locatelli and I had done together, so that gave us a fantastic leg up. It was ironic really, because before it went into administration the board of the old company had only really wanted to keep me on in order to take advantage of the television series, and now I was getting the benefit myself!

Next we had to work out what to do with the remaining restaurants, which to be honest, weren't really up to the standard of Borough Market. Andrew felt that the Fish! brand was no longer right for them, and I had to agree. By coincidence we did have another brand available – and oddly enough, it was also something that had sprung from the television series. When Giorgio Locatelli and I were filming we had such a good time that the obvious thing to do was open a restaurant together. So I set up a company called Loco Restaurants Ltd for us to open a restaurant called Loco. But before we had a chance to get any further with it, everything was going pear-shaped with Fish! and I was too tied up in the administration process to do anything about opening a restaurant with Giorgio. So, with Giorgio's permission, Loco Restaurants ended up being the shell company that was used to buy back Fish!.

Giorgio had decided to go off and do his own projects, so we were left with the 'Loco' brand going spare. So in January 2003 we decided to have an experiment in creating a simple family-style Italian neighbourhood restaurant, to be called Loco. We used the old Surbiton branch of Fish! as our first one – closed it down, restyled it, and reopened it as Loco with a very inviting menu of fantastic but accessible Italian food. Even though he wasn't directly involved, Giorgio Locatelli was such a good friend to me with the project and helped me find the staff, and especially the chef, Nick Melmouth Coombs. The whole thing only took about two weeks, and the new Surbiton Loco traded very well from the start.

Next we took a look at our Blackheath restaurant, which had had a varied life over the years, but had always done pretty well, no matter what. The Blackheath site was the one which had been done quickly as 'Lawn', a suburban version of Bank, way back when we had first become a public company. By now it had become a Fish! branch, and we had had offers for the site, but we felt it had a lot of mileage as another Loco. So we converted it to a

Loco and opened in March 2003. That has been a very successful conversion for us, and we have also incorporated our head office into the site. The restaurant itself is very cost effective because it is only open half the week. We do five nights in the back half of the week and lunches as well at weekends and it has taken off fantastically. Mind you, some of the residents are less thrilled because it so busy! We would love to add on an extension for a veranda and an outdoor terrace for the summer, but even though they love to eat there, the locals don't want it any busier.

All through this period from January 2003 through to the end of March, when we were converting restaurants and getting back on our feet again, the television series was running on BBC2. With Giorgio being involved, a lot of the food we were discussing and cooking was Italian, and I think that was one of the things that helped the Surbiton and Blackheath Locos get off to such a good start. The timing couldn't have worked better. Our County Hall site was still a Fish!, but the Loco name was doing so well now that we reopened County Hall as a Loco. It is open all day offering very simple good value Italian dishes that go down really well with all the tourists visiting that part of the South Bank. We had started buzzing again very quickly – to the extent where we felt able to open a new restaurant.

There was an outlet next door to Fish! at Borough Market that was part of our lease. I knew I could do something with it, and it was opportunity to experiment with a concept which has been close to my heart for a long time, which is that takeaway food doesn't have to be junk food. I think you should be able to go and buy a pizza or fish and chips to take away that is every bit as good quality and fresh as if you had it in a restaurant. I have never really understood why fast food compromises on quality in the way it does. So on the new site we opened up a takeaway pizzeria called Loco Pronto, which serves excellent Roman-style flat pizzas, every bit as good as a pizza you would get on holiday in Italy.

That meant we had three Loco restaurants and a Loco Pronto up and running – but before you could really call it a chain, we received an offer for the Surbiton Loco. We had really only just got Surbiton going, but it was such a good offer – about £250,000 – that we really had to accept it. Even after the refurbishment costs and everything, it still represented a profit of about £80,000, which in our position, just getting started again, we would have been very foolish to refuse. At the same time I had been offered a restaurant site in Fulham. It was an excellent location that I was excited about, and really wanted. Selling Surbiton meant that we were able to roll the proceeds straight into buying the Fulham site, which quickly became the next Loco.

It was scarcely 18 months since Andrew Cohen and I had bought the company back, and already we were establishing a much more viable business. Our activities were more stream-lined, the whole set up was neater and more cost efficient. Plus we had been able to gain the freeholds on many of our properties, for example, Jarvis retail fishmongers in Kingston-upon-Thames, and Fulham Loco, so we had a lot more security. And of course, by now our three core restaurants – Fish! Borough Market and the Locos in Fulham and Blackheath – were doing very well. So in the end it didn't work out too badly at all! What seemed like a disaster at the time that Fish! went under has probably turned out to be the makings of a fabulous deal for me now that the business has re-emerged and come through it all.

Yet I've received a fair amount of criticism about what happened, mainly from the financial press. A lot of people will say privately that as soon as I realized I could go skint, I funked it and bottled out of the company. But that doesn't take into account that Fish! was very healthy when I passed on the reins. Some City analysts like to hint that I engineered the whole thing – which is even more ridiculous. I had spent most of my adult life getting the business to the point where it was a successful plc. Of course I wasn't going to let that disintegrate overnight, for personal pride, if for no other reason.

But that's the City for you; they love their gossip and rumour-mongering. I gather people were going round saying that I'd made a bet that I could buy Fish! back. And in January of 2003 there was a broker who wrote on a website that he wouldn't be investing in a Tony Allan company again. Those guys are their own worst enemies because they end up believing their own hype. I found it a very strange, surreal world to step into. As an entrepreneur, you are basically just an average bloke who has come up with a good idea and needs a bit of backing to make it fly. But these guys in the City, there is really no concrete, productive basis to their work. In my case, for example, they are listening to my presentation, but they don't care about restaurants or food, it's just an opportunity to move money around. For me, at the end of a day's work, I can go home thinking, 'Well, I've had a great day, I've opened two restaurants today.' But I often used to ask myself about the analysts and the brokers, 'What's their product?' I would be looking at them during a presentation, and thinking, 'I wonder what the hell it is you actually do?'

It was doing the presentations that used to get to me most. I would go in and basically tell it how it was, and if it turned out to be a good story, as Cutty's and Bank and Fish! all were, well that was just because that's how it was. But the brokers would go away and put their own spin on it. I know this is all sales technique, and I'm not against sales techniques – but there's a point where it becomes over-selling. You would talk to an analyst and whatever you told him, he'd turn it into this fucking novel. Maybe you might say something like, 'I was at Billingsgate this morning buying fish', which is something I've done almost every day of my adult life. By the time the story's been turned round it becomes: 'Tony Allan got up at an extraordinary hour to go and buy forty million pounds worth of fish and he bought so and so and ...'. There was one analyst who had obviously missed his vocation as a dramatist, because whatever you said, this guy would write what he would write. I used to think of him as a kind of 'fantasy stockbroker'. But that's the City game of Chinese whispers that ends up with over-selling and over-hyping of shares. You would tell them exactly what you were planning to do, and what you read afterwards was some kind of fantasy novel. I found it was quite a difficult thing to handle sometimes. I would be meeting people like that, and sometimes I would go away from the meeting with this weird feeling. I would imagine what I would be thinking if I could step out of my own skin and look down at myself, and I realized I would have actually asked the question: 'What the hell are you doing?'

It's that whole City merry-go-round that puts me off the idea of floating again. If I did float again, I don't think the City would reject me, because at the end of the day I have always had good concepts and the numbers have always been right. But I wouldn't do it the same way – not with my heart and soul like it was before. It would have to be a much more impersonal thing; I can honestly say at this moment in time that I wouldn't stay with it myself. I don't think I'd have an ongoing role. I would be the one to get everything ready for floatation and then I wouldn't stay a part of it. What I have learnt from the experience is that I have discovered that life after flotation just doesn't interest me. You get to know yourself better and I can admit to myself that it is hard for me to maintain my interest in projects once they have become well-established. I can find it quite hard to motivate myself these days, and I can see now that I get easily bored!

Obviously there are a number of lessons you learn going through everything that I went through with Fish!, but it's also quite important not to beat yourself up about it. Since I have bought Fish! back I haven't dwelt on the past. I didn't look back and say to myself, I wish I had done this and I wish I had done that. One question I do ask myself from time to time is whether I would have bought the company back if it hadn't been for Andrew and that conversation I had with him. I think ultimately, yes I would have – either on my own or perhaps I would have approached Christian Delteil to come in with me. And I'm still left with the question of what should I have done from the time the company originally floated. In retrospect I can see that the City, and to an extent my own board of directors, started dictating quite early on where they thought things should go, and I found myself being pulled along with it.

Should I have thrown my toys out of the pram as early as late 2000 and got rid of a load of directors? There is an argument that says I should have gone to the stock exchange, given a profits warning there and then, and immediately started a year-long back-to-basics plan. I could have spent 18 months consolidating where I would have concentrated on the brand while expanding very selectively. Then I would have been able to maximize the return from the early units – and that would certainly have been possible. Because there was never really any problem with the bottom line, with the actual numbers coming out of the business. The majority of the restaurants were either making good money or had the potential to, if properly managed. It was the internal politics that were going wrong. I felt that a few individuals had seen the chance to make a lot of money very quickly, without necessarily being committed to the long term future of the restaurants themselves. So probably with hindsight, when Ronnie left would have been the time to go in and clear everybody out and really grab hold of running the company again.

But one of the important lessons of entrepreneurship is that you can't regret in hindsight – it's a waste of time. As they say in the stock market: 'You can't job backwards'. Maybe I did go on a bit of a PR ego trip with the company in the early days, but you can't change your personality, and I have learnt that as an entrepreneur I am probably more of a sprinter than a steeplechaser or a steady long distance runner. Even at the time, in my heart of hearts, I didn't believe I was the person to take it all the way. I just wasn't temperamentally suited to be the chairman, to be in and out of institutions all day long, to be talking to bankers. I didn't like the direction the company was going. It turned into a machine. But I didn't say anything. Looking back, I now realize how completely and utterly exhausted I was by the start of the millennium. There had been this huge pressure from the board and the City to get ten restaurants open in a year and we had done eleven. Then everyone turned round and said, 'Oh, you've opened too many.' I thought, I can't get over you guys.

One of the personal issues for me was that I hadn't had a brilliant idea for a couple of years. Oh, I had plenty of ideas – which a lot of people maybe thought were brilliant, because the City was still assuming that the golden boy couldn't fail. But they weren't good enough as far as I was concerned, and inside I felt a lot of frustration. I am at my best with my back against the wall, fire-fighting, working however many hours a day it takes to get a project off the ground. And that's a very different type of demand from the mentality that can turn up and sit behind the desk signing documents and reading the *Financial Times*. Maybe it was a mistake to relax and take a little time for myself. Who knows – I probably just had too much time to think and started beating myself up over not feeling inspired. But I had high standards, I wanted to stay on that roll, and not being able to, I felt blocked.

I suppose you could say that the whole experience has given me a lot better self-knowledge – some people would say I've learned my limitations! So when I was considering floating again the other day, I moved away from the idea because my personal theories of how to make a business successful are not really 'City' theories. I believe in sticking to fundamentals: you keep your cost base low and you invest your energy and expertise in the product. I make sure I give the consumer noticeably better fish than they've ever had before. Keep the overheads low so that you can supply that better product at competitive prices, and it works. Get your basic product right, and stay in tune with it. In my case that product is fish. Whatever I do within the catering and restaurant industry, everything seems to come back to fish all the time. That's happening again already with the future projects I have lined up. I suppose it is partly because I have never really given up on my mission to get the public eating fish.

My big idea at the moment is a concept called Fish! Kitchen, and really it is cherry picking all the best elements of my previous enterprises. Obviously it is fish-based, which is great because that is what I know best – and it is also what the public keep turning back to. As a nation we have never really lost our taste for the great British fish and chips. For six years now I've had to listen to the press saying our national dish is chicken tikka masala. Giorgio and I even made a joke out of it. On the cover of our book, I'm quoted as saying how much I like English food, for example, spaghetti bolognese and pizza! But ironically fish and chips is taking off again. We're a very fickle race because just as cod is beginning to get scarce, the British suddenly want it again. That's typical of us as a nation really; we wait until something has run out before we start wanting it again.

The idea behind Fish! Kitchen is very simple, and builds on the cost-effective theories of ease of service and low staffing levels that I used in my other restaurants. I think of it as my phoenix out of the fire. We opened the first Fish! Kitchen in the autumn of 2005 in Kingston-upon-Thames, next door to Jarvis fishmongers. I am hoping it will be the start of a chain of what will be little brothers to the Borough Market Fish!, based around good fish and chips with very simply cooked fresh fish on the grill. When I think about Fish! Kitchen I find that I've got that hunger, that buzz about me again. Partly that's because it's returning to that product I know so well. I don't think there's a job I haven't done within the fish and catering industry, apart from actually going out on the trawlers I suppose! But what is really exciting me is that it gives me the opportunity to do something radical and new in the fast food area.

I hadn't realized quite how expensive ordinary takeaway food has become. You know if you order a pizza or you go and pick up some fish and chips, you aren't going to have much change from a tenner. That aspect of it interests me from a business point of view, because I think there is a niche in the market to provide excellent quality at very competitive prices – just as there was when I originally started Cutty's. For example, one of the things we have been very careful about is the packaging that our fish and chips comes in. We've tested it for a long time, and put a lot of effort into getting a packaging material that makes sure the chips don't go soggy. We've come up with a particular design of waxed paper boxes in a nice shape, so the fish can lie properly and with holes in the boxes so you don't get condensation on the inside of the box. It makes it a much nicer experience eating straight from the box.

Another good business point is that the units are cheap and quick to do. No more three-quarter of a million pound refits like we used to do in the boom times. And now that our children are growing up, Denys is able to pick up her interior design skills again and get involved in the design work. So in a way we have come full circle – back to fish as a core product, and to working with people who are close to us. I know instinctively that it's the right thing to do, but also the figures bear it out. It's important to remember that none of the ingredients of the original success story really needed to be changed. Borough Market Fish!, for example, has always been successful all the way through, and by the end of 2005 it had actually had its most profitable year since it first opened. So the evidence all points to Fish! Kitchen having the right formula for success – a strong, simple concept backed up by a lot of past experience.

I'm very confident that Fish! Kitchen will take off and we are now looking at the next sites. I really want to get out into Essex – Loughton, Epping, Chigwell. All those Essex jokes back in the 80s have led to it being an underrated county, but it has actually got an amazing eating-out culture. You can go out on a Monday night in Essex and the restaurants are full. And there is a positive attitude toward fish, partly because of the East End connection.

When I used to be spending so much time at Billingsgate it was always noticeable that about 70 per cent of the people there were Essex-based. I'm also considering that it might be a good area to test-bed the idea of a Fish! Kitchen as a franchise operation. I think the concept would be an ideal blue-print for that kind of business, although you have to be very careful to keep the standards up among the franchisees.

It was a great moment opening Fish! Kitchen in Kingston. I got that great feeling that I hadn't had with the plc of being where I was meant to be. Fish! Kitchen only had 36 seats, but for the launch party we had a guest list of 750, and that was cutting it back to the bare minimum. And because the concept is basically proven, you don't have that pressure of whether or not it will work. A lot of my old team from the days of Cutty's and Bank are back with me as well, though one of the people I would love to work with again is Christian Delteil, whose career since Bank has taken off tremendously well. But I think the next project now will be to open another Fish! branch, rather than Fish! Kitchen. I want to develop the two names alongside each other, with Fish! as the overall flag-ship and Fish! Kitchen as its little brother. I'd like to do probably two more Fish! branches and then develop anything between six to ten Fish! Kitchens, keeping them very simple in style so they would require a minimum of centralized management. So as far as managing and getting the bought-back business straightened out, streamlined and profitable again, it's good to know that it's in a great position at the moment. But I can't honestly see myself going down the flotation route again. I value my family life too much to take us all back onto that roller-coaster ride of the last 20 years – though the idea of a franchise operation of 50 or 60 simple fish restaurants might still tempt me.

Chapter Nine

The Supermodel Chefs

I
T IS 25 years since I first stepped through the door into that incredible kitchen at Claridges, with all those chefs running around in their white aprons and their tall starched hats. A quarter of a century, and the way we eat has changed tremendously. The restaurant and catering industry has had to move constantly to adapt to that. I'm always impressed by how certain figures within the business have been able to lead the way and dictate the pace of change. Back when I started, everything was 'fine dining' – gourmet food if you like. The most fashionable restaurants were always the Michelin starred ones. Getting a Michelin star could make a restaurant and a chef's name, but oddly enough it could also break him. That's why I've never been an advocate of the Michelin guide. I have seen too many chefs treated like culinary gods for very little reason, and I have also seen too many businesses go by the wayside when they went down the Michelin route. In my career I have gone from wanting to have every Michelin restaurant as a client, to getting close to those restaurants and seeing how the quest for stars can end up destroying a business.

The problem with going for Michelin stars has always been what it does to the bottom line of your business. You get the situation of a rising young chef, with a very nice 30-seat restaurant, who is doing fabulous food, very natural and original cooking, and pretty soon he gets noticed. Then the Michelin guys come and he gets his first star. Then along comes the second star and everything is wonderful and he's being tipped for three stars – and then the next thing you know he's gone skint. The trouble is that you have to have a hell of a lot of finance, or a big hotel, behind you to go down the Michelin star route, because the overheads become so huge. Food presentation, for example, is a major part of what the Michelin guys are looking for. So perhaps you might have a very nice dish on your menu with sea bass. What Michelin will be looking for is this perfect square shape of sea bass sitting on its little *jus* with all its garnishes. But that's not how you find a sea bass swimming in the sea! You might only get four of those perfect square fillets out of a bass, so there's a hell of a lot of wastage, which is expensive. That's why there will always be very, very few Michelin 3-star restaurants in this country.

It is a different situation in Europe and especially in France. They have a completely different relationship with food from the British. Here we take food for granted, but in France they are very close to it – to the actual produce that goes into making great dishes. Every village and town has its baker, a butcher, the charcuterie, a fishmonger. And those are the guys everybody in the village respects, forget the stockbrokers and the car mechanics. At the top of it all of course, is the local restaurant, especially if it's got a Michelin star or two. It is such a completely different hierarchy from here.

But there is one thing that has made an even greater impact on the restaurant industry than Michelin and that is the recession of the late 80s and early 90s, which profoundly changed the way restaurateurs thought. It even ended up changing the public's taste in food. There was a lack of disposable income around and it was very hard to make any money from a gourmet menu. Expensive ingredients like lobster, truffles and foie gras were too high an overhead to carry when you could no longer guarantee full restaurants every night. So chefs really had to dig deep and do some gutsy innovative cooking. That sorted the men from the boys, and you saw really good cooks like Mark Hix at Le Caprice coming through. He was able to adapt. In the past his menu would have had dishes using Scotch lobster and truffles, but instead he produced wonderful new ideas with basic produce like cod and lentils. Watching what he was doing made me realize that from a business point of view, restaurateurs and their suppliers – which meant me and Cutty's – had to be quick to adapt to changing market conditions.

For me though, the most important thing to come out of the recession was the rise of Terence Conran and the gastrodome. Conran really got going just as we were coming out of the recession in about 1991. He was so innovative. He was thinking outside the box, and instead of carrying on with the old style of fine dining restaurant that we all knew from the 80s, he applied some general business practices – one of which was how to make economies of scale. Instead of having a 30 or 40 seat restaurant that needed to serve high value, high mark-up food to cover its overheads, he turned a corner, and suddenly there were a lot more seats in restaurants. And in these bigger restaurants people didn't need to spend so much per head for it to work. I'm one of Terence Conran's storm troopers. I won't have a bad word said about him. What he has done for London eating is brilliant. He took somewhere like Butler's Wharf, which was basically just a wartime bomb site, and turned it into a gastrodome. The large brasserie-style of restaurant which he pioneered has a completely different approach to eating out. The food doesn't rely on expensive ingredients, so that cost doesn't have to be passed on to the customer. And the whole atmosphere of his restaurants is different. They are accessible to people who wouldn't dream of booking a table at a Michelin star restaurant. We take this style of restaurant for granted now, but I firmly believe Terence Conran was the pioneer. It is always difficult to be the first. Usually in our business you look at what the public want and try to give it to them, but Conran decided the public didn't know what it wanted until he had given it to them – and that takes balls.

It had a big impact on me too, because it helped create a huge demand for the service I was providing with Cutty's. All the restaurant kitchens were de-skilling, and increasing the number of covers they served every day – which meant they had no time to do their own fish preparation. Nor did they have chefs with the ability to do it. I remember Mezzo restaurant once sent 18 sous chefs down to us at Cutty's for training in fish preparation. Now a sous chef is basically the second-in-command rank in the kitchen, and in my day it would have taken ten years to get to that level. But the skills had gone out of the industry to such an extent that Mezzo had guys who couldn't even take a salmon off the bone. It meant that a company like Cutty's that could buy fish, prepare it, cut it into portions the way a chef would, and then sell it to these places that were doing 1200 or 1500 covers a week, had a ready-made market. At Le Caprice they were serving 400 people a day, and The Ivy was doing 450. For them there was a major skill problem and at Cutty's we pioneered the pre-preparation service that enabled kitchens to be de-skilled successfully. If you take a fashionable top West End restaurant like Quaglino's, for example, in the past they would have had their fish section and butchery section and larder work, just like I used to do at Claridges. That would have meant a kitchen employing about 140 chefs, yet Quaglino's runs on about 40 or 50 kitchen staff. Cutty's made that possible by doing not only the pre-prepared fish, but also nearly all the poultry. And we supplied all the specialized stuff like truffles and duck legs, so in a way we were responsible for a hell of a lot of the menu.

I don't think it was a coincidence that this was roughly the period where you saw the rise of the celebrity chef. It was a case of the ingredients no longer being so important – if the food wasn't doing the talking, then the chef himself had to be the unique selling proposition. There was a culinary explosion in London after the recession, and this time the chefs were the superstars. There used to be this stereotype of what a chef looked like – the big fat pot-bellied French guy in the tall hat and apron. Now you had some good-looking young guy with long hair, no hat and his jacket undone. Chefs were suddenly supermodels, they were on magazine covers. There was Gary Rhodes at The Castle, and Gary Holyhead, who was at Sutherland's in Soho, and David Cavalier who had his own place, Cavalier's. And they brought a breath of fresh air to the trade. And of course, that's where Marco Pierre White came in. He was such a new face on the scene, and the way he revolutionized the world of restaurant PR was unbelievable. Marco was a pioneer of this young chef/patron style that was coming in and I was more than happy to be a part of it.

The thing that Marco did that was very clever – which I noticed right from the start, because I knew him from very early on – was that he would learn from people. In a short space of time at the beginning of his career, Marco worked for the four top kitchens. He worked for Pierre Kauffman, Raymond Blanc, Nico Ladenis, and Albert Roux, and he took away a skill from each experience. From Albert Roux he learned business acumen. Albert was a very shrewd businessman, and Marco quickly realized that as a restaurateur it is not enough just to be a good cook – you have to be able to run a business as well. Then from Pierre Kauffman he took on board some wonderful gutsy cooking skills. Pierre was this great rustic, down to earth, fantastically skilful cook, whose dishes everybody loved. So that was the food element for Marco. Working with Raymond Blanc gave him the opportunity to discover the importance of how you present the food. Raymond has a tremendous artistic flair, so that a meal at one of his restaurants is like a piece of theatre, and Marco saw the importance of that. And of course, with Nico Ladenis he learnt about being outspoken! So in a way you could say that Marco the finished article ended up being an amalgam of all the best attributes of the leading guys within the restaurant scene in London – and that's how Marco moulded himself. What Marco could do beyond anything was reinvent the wheel. He'd take the idea of a dish from someone else, and you would think he was doing it exactly the same, but somehow he just made it so much better. Marco is a very instinctive cook.

We developed a close relationship over the years, but it wasn't always easy being Marco's mate. He needed you there for him, and you would say the things he wanted to hear. But I think he was always getting so much adulation that he did get rather spoilt. He would want his own way and he demanded quite a lot from his friends – the 2am phone calls were the worst! But even though he could be a difficult person, I have always thought of Marco as one of the great cooks. And of course, having a mercurial temperament goes with the territory for superstar chefs. These guys made food sexy, so today when you make the big time as a chef, the first thing that happens is that you start seeing your face on the front of magazines. Marco and the others turned chefs from being cooks into something more like professional footballers. Their position very much compares with being a premier league footballer, where you are a star in your own right. A chef who sees his name in lights for the first time, who is suddenly getting that sort of wealth, is just like a young footballer with a new club, and you need to have a lesson in social skills. Most chefs probably haven't got hundreds of exams and academic qualifications behind them, and a lot of what you do is instinctive. With a footballer it's his feet, and with a chef it's the food – but you get put up on a pedestal for it, far too early in life. It's ridiculous.

As a chef you are running your kitchen, but you go out into the restaurant at the end of the evening – and the women are waiting for you! It's, 'Oh, do come over to our table', and they are all over you. I'm not quite sure of the attraction of some sweaty chef straight out of the kitchen, but the clients do like you coming out, so if you are a chef/patron, you think, 'Well, I'd better go out', and naturally the first thing you do is talk to the good-looking women. The women really went for Marco and they would all be flirting, 'Oh, Marco came out and spoke to me.' It was always the best-looking woman and they could be completely outrageous. There aren't that many people who can cope with all the adulation, and that's where the temperament comes into it. And there are other aspects that are difficult – especially in an industry like the restaurant business, where the hours are so antisocial. Temptations are rife in the business.

You get the combination of the unsocial hours combined with a lot of stress and pressure to perform. As far as the business is concerned, any chef is only as good as his last plate of food. And in the kitchen you are working to these ridiculous deadlines, trying to get four or five hundred or more dishes out to the diners in time without complaints or mix ups. Again it's like football. If you have a bad game you know there's a risk you won't get in the side the following week. It's the same for a chef. If you cook an important meal for a restaurant critic and you get a shit review, you know the business will go down in the restaurant. I think all this combines to produce the sort of very temperamental and prima donna attitudes you see in the business. Everybody knows which chefs are the ones that will fly off the handle. Gordon Ramsay has built a whole TV series around whether or not he uses the f-word! There was a time when Gordon needed to mend his image, where I think he was overdoing it. It is easy for young would-be chefs to be put off going into the industry. But the thing people need to remember about chefs is that usually their bark is worse than their bite and you shouldn't take too much notice of it. Like Raymond Blanc. He's a very passionate man and people might say he's temperamental, but he cares so much about food.

Nico Ladenis is another everybody remembers for going into a rage if a diner asked for the salt, and that was part of the whole experience of eating at one of his restaurants. I remember a very poignant moment back in the late 80s. Nico and I were chatting one night, and he was saying, 'You know, Tony, it's gonna be a tough year this year.' And then he turned to me with this little grin, and he said: 'One thing we have to remember is we aren't going to be able to throw them out any more – we need them now!' It made me realize he wasn't someone who took himself as seriously as people think he did. And Nico was one of the few who did get his third Michelin star. He waited a long time for it, because I don't think he started cooking professionally until he was in his mid-30s. People in the industry were being bitchy about it, but I thought it was very much deserved. He really did earn that third star. With the great chefs, I think you have to accept some prima donna behaviour, but the trouble is that some of the up-and-coming chefs believe they have to imitate it because they think it's going to help their business. That's understandable too. The restaurant industry can be so up-and-down. Everybody eats food, everybody's got an opinion on cooking, and all sorts of people are trying to set themselves up as experts. There's so much gossip as well. You get people talking behind your back all the time. Then there is the whole problem of getting your kitchen staff to come through for you. You might be the greatest Michelin chef around, but if you can't communicate that to your team and get them to come up with what you want, then you haven't done your job properly. It's one of those no-win situations where you are being judged all the time, yet you are dependent on other people to help you come up with the goods. It's very frustrating. The kitchen is a pressure cooker environment, so you are bound to get explosions!

From the moment when I became a fishmonger and restaurateur, rather than a full-time chef, I haven't missed life in the kitchen. In fact I have actually become a better cook since coming out of the kitchen. A lot of English chefs tend to get pigeon-holed in one area. Back in the 80s and into the 90s chefs were working all hours. They never had the opportunity to get out and discover different kinds of cuisine. But as a supplier, and eating at a hell of a lot of restaurants, it changed a lot of my theories about what I liked. I came full circle, back to the kind of straightforward food I enjoyed as a kid. You go from Claridges and the Dorchester, which is over-indulgence on a plate, to enjoying very simple stuff. For a lot of chefs actually, you'll find they eat oriental food when they are not cooking – that's holiday food! Even though I stopped cooking full time, I had to eat at a lot of customers' restaurants. These guys all had their Michelin stars and wanted to show what they could do. I remember Richard Neat had two Michelin stars at Pied a Terre and we'd all gone to eat there. So Richard was sending out taster after taster – the *amuses bouches* – which come before you even get to your starter. I'd had so many *amuses* that I barely touched the entrée. I was stuffed, my palate was in total confusion and I ended up saying to the waiter, 'I just can't manage any more'. So Denys and I were driving back home to Kent, and I was thinking about how I was going to have to be up in a couple of hours to go off to Billingsgate. Then the next thing, Richard is on the phone telling me how offended he is that I have left food on my plate, that I won't eat his food. He's threatening to withdraw his fish order because I have insulted him. Crazy things used to happen all the time.

Although it sounds very glamorous – eating out every night, always being able to get a table at the most fashionable restaurants – it didn't really feel like that at the time. In some ways the period of Cutty's taking off and everything, from about '87 through to '92, was in many ways the worst period of my life. There would be phone calls at midnight. A lot of the time it was Marco, and we would end up talking till all hours. And everything else was going on; the restaurant kitchens would be wanting stuff all the time. On the plus side it was a very social life, but the downside was that one of the compulsory things that we had to do was we eat out at our customers' restaurants all the time, and that was a burden sometimes. Over that period I don't think I can remember eating an evening meal at home. And if Ronnie Truss and I were going to a new restaurant, it was quite a performance. The gossip would be, 'Oh Tony's taken his wife to such and such place.' Or at the restaurant the word would go back to the kitchen, 'The fishmongers are in with their families.' And then you couldn't just have a quiet meal.

But there was one new restaurant we went to visit that turned out to be special. I remember Ronnie used to come into the office at Cutty's every morning and we used to meet. This one day, it must have been in about 1990, Ronnie came in and said he'd heard about this Italian, this mad Italian guy with long hair, at this little restaurant in Victoria called Olivo. So we went over to try this guy's food and I took the chef of the Caprice with me, Mark Hix. It was throwing it down with rain, and we came in to this little 36-seat restaurant, all done in wonderful Sardinian colours – a lot of bright yellow and deep blues – with very simple brick walls. And this was Giorgio Locatelli's first restaurant in London. The food was brilliant, absolutely brilliant, but when I looked at the menu I realized that it was the most recession-based menu I'd ever seen. That's the way I looked at it as an Englishman, but it was the produce that Giorgio had grown up with in Italy. For him the recession didn't come into it – that was his food. The place was humming, but I think the most expensive fish he had on the menu was a sardine! And he had a dish on with pig's liver. In England pig's liver is what you give the cat when it's been poorly. Denys and I and Mark Hix and his wife all had a great meal, and I was gob-smacked at his food. So I went into the kitchen to see Giorgio afterwards. We just had so much in common and immediately forged our friendship. About a year later Giorgio wanted to open another restaurant and it was an obvious thing for me to back him. But I had also happened to introduce Giorgio to Claudio Pulzi who launched The Canteen with Marco Pierre White and Michael Caine. It wasn't too long before Claudio and Giorgio had opened Zafarano together, so I missed out. Fair play to them. I went off and did Bank, and it was to be quite a few years before we ended up fulfilling our aim of working together.

It was fabulous to have the opportunity to do the TV series with Giorgio. He is one of the chefs I have always enjoyed working with, right up alongside Christian Delteil, who was my head chef at Bank. If I was to do another big restaurant project Christian would be first on the list of people I would want on board. Alongside Christian and Giorgio, I think the chef I rate most highly has to be Mark Hix. His work at the Ivy and Le Caprice has been fantastic, and of course he's now one of the co-owners of that restaurant group. These guys are all chefs who are also restaurateurs, but what makes them good is that they remain chefs first. Their passion for produce and cooking is what puts them in a different league. It is more than 20 years since The Ivy and Le Caprice became among the most fashionable restaurants in London, and they are still up there now. Jeremy King and Chris Corbin who opened them, along with Sheekeys, are world champions – the Steve Redgraves of the industry.

But one of the best of all the restaurants is about as far from London as you can get – and that's Rick Stein's restaurant at Padstow in Cornwall. It was actually Keith Floyd who originally launched Rick. He had him appearing in his Floyd on Fish series. Then I got to know Rick well in the 80s because he used to come up and do demonstrations for Cutty's at the various food shows and at Olympia. Rick is fantastic. Partly his talent lies in the fact that his own tastes are very simple, so his cooking just lets the wonderful produce – the fish – stand for itself. He's very passionate about his locale down there in Cornwall, and he is lucky that he can use the fish that comes in each day straight off the boats. Unfortunately the chefs working further inland don't have that available to them, but I was very influenced by Rick in my desire to bring sea-fresh fish to everyone – even those not lucky enough to live near Brixham or Padstow. Rick has had great PR through being a chef that has made the industry wake up to the importance of fresh, high-quality ingredients, but he has also kept coming up with the goods year after year. That's another important quality of a top chef: that they maintain the same high standards that originally got them noticed. I think Rick is in a league of his own really, but one chef I would compare him with in terms of consistency is Gary Rhodes.

Gary is very much a chef's chef, he's very technical. He's had his Michelin star restaurants and he always produces superb, quite classic British food – lovely clean-tasting stuff, no muddled flavours. I think the only criticism I would make is that his books are maybe a bit too technical for amateur chefs. I think my mum, for example, would get pretty stressed doing a Gary Rhodes recipe. But then at the other end of the spectrum you have Jamie Oliver, and I think my mum would find his books equally hard to follow. He's taking a dollop of this and a drizzle of that, and my mum would be wondering exactly how much a drizzle is. But then Jamie's a very instinctive cook, whereas Gary is much more classical. Some people think Jamie is overdoing all this natural cooking, and that maybe he's putting it on a bit for the cameras. In fact that's just the way he is. His way of cooking just comes from a feel for the ingredients. Jamie's rise to fame has been unusual because he had a TV series before he even had his own restaurant. He was spotted bouncing around the kitchen at the River Café doing his thing, and that's how he got his break.

People in the industry were knocking him for that, saying he had no real experience. But he had the bottle to get out there and do it and get his message across, and he is a great natural, gutsy cook. For television viewers he was a breath of fresh air. When Giorgio and I were commissioned to do our TV series I didn't know much about what was on telly at the time because I was always working. So I started to watch the TV chef and lifestyle programmes and do a bit of research into their ratings. It was interesting to see that things had got a bit stale with the lifestyle strand – food, gardening, DIY. Gary Rhodes's ratings were steady but Delia Smith's were actually dropping. *Ready, Steady, Cook* was holding its own – and that show has a good formula because it is constantly changing within its basic format. Nigella Lawson's ratings were more or less non-existent. It's a shame. She's so sexy, but I think that actually counted against her. When her show went to America apparently her ratings actually went down because guys were staying in to watch her and their wives were getting annoyed. But I'm not sure I would class Nigella as a true chef in a professional sense. I think I'd put her more in the category of dinner party cooks, a sort of trendy Sophie Grigson.

But the point is that many of our very best chefs don't appear on television anyway. The only chef I've ever been really envious of is Nobu Matsuhisa, who has the Nobu chain of Japanese restaurants. I first came across him when I was in Los Angeles, before the court case. Vinnie Jones was filming in Hollywood and he was wanted on set, so I had some spare time and went for a stroll through Beverly Hills and that's when I came across Nobu. The Nobu Beverly Hills is just a little café really, compared with the restaurants he has now at the Metropolitan on Park Lane and at Canary Wharf, but it was just incredible. When he opened Nobu at the Met about a year before we opened Bank, I have to admit I was jealous. For a start the restaurant itself was so stylish, very cosmopolitan and not as Japanese as I thought it would be. Then, as a businessman, I could see that the bums on seats side of it really worked – he had a tremendous through-put of diners. All this was before I actually started eating. I went through the first five or six dishes on the menu, and it is very rare to see a restaurant menu with that amount of consistently mind blowing dishes. I had the sashimi salad and then the black cod, then the rock shrimp, and I thought, Christ Almighty. The tastes were so unbelievably clean and defined. I looked at the whole thing, and what Nobu had achieved was brilliant. I've got so much respect for him as a restaurateur. Nobu's are probably the only restaurants that I admire 100 per cent.

But there are a few others that would go on my top ten list, especially the ones with legs, that go on producing great food and good atmosphere consistently. Obviously Le Caprice, The Ivy, and Langan's Brasserie would all fit in that category, as does Rules. Sheekey's is another that is right up there. I like Tim Hughes, who is the head chef there at the moment and who used to work for me at Bank. He could be a temperamental chef though. He used to beat himself up mentally if he felt he was falling short, and that used to make him an angry man – but a great character. The Pont de la Tour is another of my favourite restaurants; I love the setting and the atmosphere there. I'm a great fan of everything that Giorgio does, so his current restaurant, Locando Locatelli, is definitely in my top ten. Hakkasan would be my other nomination inside London, which was started by Alan Yau one of the original guys that started the Wagamama chain, which is one of my favourites in the fast food category. Outside London, the Fat Duck at Bray takes a lot of beating, and a lot of people would agree, as it's on its third star now.

Some people would criticize me for choosing a Terence Conran restaurant – Le Pont de la Tour – because to some pundits, Conran is a dirty word. They think of him as someone just rolling out an image rather than being interested in food. But I don't think you can raise that as a criticism because Terence has never set out to be a chef/patron. He is a designer first and foremost, so nobody goes to his restaurants expecting him to cook. What I do have a problem with is the chefs who open a lot of restaurants using their name as a brand. Nico Ladenis was among the first of the chefs who became a brand-name. I've got a lot of time for Nico and I'm a great fan of his personal cooking. I think he's a great character too – I can remember we met through him throwing me out of his restaurant, and I still ended up getting his fish order.

We all have to make a living, and most of the top chefs are doing similar deals. Gordon Ramsay is involved with a load of restaurants, but if I wanted to eat Gordon Ramsay food the only one I would bother going to is his original Royal Hospital Road restaurant, that's the one with three Michelin stars. I think Gordon would be the first to say himself, he's been jetted out to Dubai and so forth, and it isn't going to be the same thing. You can't spread yourself that thin and expect to do the same style of food throughout. There's a lot of debate within the industry about whether this new style of 'flying chef' is a rip off or not. I take the view that it both is and isn't. I think it is a rip-off if the public go to a restaurant being led to expect one thing, and they don't get it, and what they get instead is a bad meal. But if it is obvious that what is on offer is a 'baby brother' – what they would call a second label in the fashion industry – or a 'touch of', then that's fair enough, particularly if it raises the standards of what might otherwise be a fairly mediocre restaurant. I think ultimately it's another case of the consumers voting with their feet. If the spin-offs are also rip-offs, people won't go.

But looking at my top ten I notice that a lot of them are quite long established. Locando Locatelli, Hakkasan and The Fat Duck are more recent, but mainly they date from what I think was pretty much the golden age for eating out through the 80s and 90s. At that time London was considered to be the culinary capital of the world. It was fantastic for me being a part of that. It was such an exciting time to be running in and out of these truly amazing restaurants, playing a real role in their menus. And then to launch my own restaurants – especially Bank and Fish! Borough Market – that were right up there with them, was such a thrill. But I think the industry is in danger of going stale. When the superstar chefs came in they did for restaurants what the supermodels did for fashion. At the moment though, we are all looking to see what the next big thing will be. The business needs something to happen again.

Chapter Ten

The Harder You Work, the Luckier You Get

PEOPLE WHO have been successful in business, and maybe made a lot of money, are always asked the key to their success. There are business schools devoted to teaching highly-qualified graduates the theoretical way of achieving entrepreneurial success. I didn't go to university and I haven't got an MBA, but over my business career I think I've done a hell of a lot more right than I've done wrong. From when I first started buying fish (and not including my teenage un-roofing activities!), I have started six major business projects: Cutty's, Bank, Quadranet, Fish!, Loco, and my property investments. Of all those enterprises, only the roll-out of Fish! wasn't completely successful. So I reckon I probably haven't done much wrong in business terms. But identifying exactly what you have done right – and particularly expressing it as a sort of business theory – is much harder.

For me, entrepreneurship has always been pretty much an instinctive thing, but if I could put my finger on just the single most important aspect of what I have done, I think it comes down to the basic idea. If your original business idea is good enough, and you believe in it – really believe in it, so that you aren't embarrassed to tell people about it – then that will take you a long way. My basic idea was obviously to trade fish in a way that hadn't been done before. It was innovative; my initial trial runs showed it could work; and I really believed passionately in it. I think it would be very hard to get started as an entrepreneur without that initial high-quality idea. To me, this is where all the business schools with their formulas tend to miss the point. They are trying to give people theories to make up for a lack of the basic idea in the first place. If your idea is good enough, all the rest – the business side of it – seems just to follow, and you learn it as you go along. That's not to say though, that the idea alone is all you need. To be successful, an entrepreneur has to have the right personal qualities, and then the good business structures have to be put in place pretty quickly.

You need to have a strong awareness of what your strengths and weaknesses are, and that can be surprisingly difficult – a lot of what I've done has been a bit of a voyage of self-discovery. I always knew that I was someone who would be absolutely focused when the project was right. And I have the ability to work really hard for long stretches. 16- or 20-hour days have been pretty much routine for me most of my working life, and when I was getting started I never even thought about taking a holiday. But no matter how hard you work, you have to recognize that you aren't going to be able to do it all on your own. That's where the next important business skill comes in: people. You have to be able to pick the right people, build a good relationship with them, and all of you have to be able to talk to each other.

I have found that the people aspect becomes more difficult to get right the bigger your business grows. I think the only way you can find good people is to go out and watch them working and if you like what they are doing, you need to offer them something worthwhile. When I started Cutty's I remembered Ronnie Truss and his energy, and I went out and tracked him down. I have been very lucky with the people I have worked with. Especially at the start of my career, it was just a handful of us – Ronnie, Christian, Jeremy and me – and we didn't waste time with lots of meetings or office politics, we were too busy getting the job done. I don't consider myself to be a difficult person to work with. I've got high standards and I don't suffer fools gladly. But I'm very straightforward. If someone has a problem, I expect them to come to me with it, and if they need help they will get it. I don't take any bullshit though, and I've always been well-known for leaving a trail of ruffled feathers behind me. I achieve a lot more than a lot of other people can, but I do like to have people to mop up after me. I used to be a lot worse, but I don't get so worked up about things any more. That kind of style works well in a small close-knit team who are working towards big rewards, but it doesn't necessarily adapt to the needs of a large, structured business like a plc.

When it comes to people skills at that level, I'm probably as guilty of making mistakes as anybody else. At the roll-out of Fish!, for example, I thought I had chosen the right people to take it forward, but perhaps my judgement was marred by the fact that I'd had enough of life with a plc at that stage. I was putting people in place, and there was a hell of a lot of money in the bank for the company, but with hindsight, obviously it didn't work. There is a pitfall that you have to be aware of when you have got to the stage of being a public company, and I think it was what caught me out at that point. Instinctively you can feel if something isn't quite right, and I think there was a part of me that very much wanted to pick up the reins again and run the team. I would have been saying, 'I want to change these things, I want to base the roll-out around the core product – exceptional quality fish and chips – and this is how we should be going forward.' The reason that didn't happen is because I had fallen into the trap of worrying about what the board's reaction would be. You get into the situation where you stop being a restaurateur and find yourself thinking like a private detective: 'What are they gonna be thinking? What will their next step be?' That's not the way it should be. I had ended up in a position where I was thinking of something – an action, an expansion plan or whatever – but first and foremost, rather than the good of the consumer and the good of the business, I was more worried about what the reaction of the City would be. Whereas in the past I would just have got on with it, I was trying to second guess everything. By not staying true to the core concept that had built my success in the first place, I lost the instinctive ability to get it right.

There are other fine lines to be trodden as your business becomes more complex. Knowing the right moment to step in and do something major can be very hard to judge. Firstly you have to avoid denial – if a situation is going pear-shaped you have to grab hold of it early on and put the project back on track. If you leave it too late, something that was only going a little bit wrong at first rapidly gets to the point where you've got a hell of a lot to make up. So catching it really early on is important. But then you have to be aware of the danger of jumping in too soon and over-correcting. It's a bit like a ship where if you over-steer one way then the other, you end up going in a zig-zag. I have watched people in business who think they have stepped in and corrected a problem early on, and have ended up doing more damage. Sometimes you are better off letting that project head towards self-destruct for a while and then bring it back from there. You have to give the business a chance to prove itself. That might mean that you just have to let it go a further distance and wait to see whether it will turn itself.

It's a very fine judgement call to make. I'm sure there are all sorts of theoretical models people learn in business school that are meant to come up with the right answer every time, but really I think you can probably only learn it through experience. What the business schools don't tell you is that things are going to go wrong from time to time, and strangely enough, that's not necessarily a bad thing. One of the attributes that has helped me immensely in launching my projects is that I am naturally quite optimistic. I've never got depressed when things went badly – even when I first got sacked or when Fish! went into administration. And it is important in business not to let yourself get despondent. Discover your self-reliance. As far as the City is concerned one of the things that has always impressed them about me is that I've always been at heart a trader. Whether it was trading fish as a product, or trading concepts, I've always got ideas and projects up and running and pumping and doing well.

What I have learnt though, especially through the experience with Fish!, is that I'm not the person to take those schemes all the way through to becoming major City institutions. That's been one of the major lessons – identify your strengths. Don't look at it romantically. The fact that you built the first one of a chain doesn't mean you are going to be there for the 250th. There are some wonderful business stories of people who got it right. Look at Peter Boizot with Pizza Express. He's always stayed a big shareholder, and he's been able to watch all the boys carry on his fantastic concept. And he had some great people in place to take it forward and run with it. I applaud him for identifying something like that and being able to take it to that other level. Maybe if there had been a Luke Johnson around for Fish!, I would now be non-executive chairman with a few shares popping into the odd board meeting of a massive national chain of fish restaurants, but that didn't happen in my case.

Maybe I personally wasn't the right person to be dealing with the board and with the City. People might criticize my communication skills – but frankly the very phrase 'communication skills' sums up everything I dislike about the City. It reminds me of endless board meetings, and copying people in, and external conferences, and all the rest of it, and basically I think that's all totally unnecessary if you're in my kind of business life. To be honest, I absolutely hate meetings, can't stand them. The majority of the time they're pointless, and invariably they are to sort out a problem which shouldn't have been there in the first place if people were doing their jobs properly – instead of having endless meetings.

Legally I know, you have to have board meetings and there has to be a certain amount of protocol, but most board meetings I've ever found myself in, it has always gone way over the top. You get good professional people and once they are in the board meeting they act as if someone's cut their tongue out because they're worried about the little guy sitting in the corner taking the minutes. Instead of getting the job done people are sitting round this massive great table and they're worried about if they've got nothing say, so they aren't going to make an appearance in the minutes. Then if they have got something to say they are thinking: is that going to be leaked and end up all over the newspapers? Or are they going to be sneered at or shouted down by the rest of the board. The whole thing is just so negative. You know the best people I've ever worked with – Christian Delteil, Eric Garnier, even Ronnie Truss – proper working directors, when it came to board meetings they rarely said anything at all. So the whole thing is absolutely completely pointless. It's always the non-executives chirping up with some meaningless remark like 'are we monitoring cash flow?' just so they get themselves in the minutes to justify being paid 30 or 40 grand a year.

The only type of meeting I do enjoy is a management meeting. It is my chance to have a proper talk with my staff – the guys who cook for me, the guys who run the restaurants. Invariably we talk about the customer coming through the door and how we can gear around the customers to give them a better experience, because the most important thing is the customers who come into the restaurant. They are meetings I enjoy because they are constructive meetings. They are about getting things done. You end up with an action plan. And if you are talking about 'communication skills', it's in these kind of meetings that you actually do express yourself a lot more. They are how you keep in touch with the grass root workers who are actually going to deliver your business plan. I prefer to be able to be very direct, at all levels in business. I've never been afraid of confrontation, and I don't think anyone needs to be. If you know you've done a good job, then confrontation isn't a problem. It only becomes difficult if you haven't followed through on your promises, and the only thing to do then is face it and accept it – that was a very important lesson I learnt right at the beginning with the fish supply business.

Although I'm not a fan of abstract business theories in the academic sense, I do think that there are practical formulas for success which apply to specific kinds of business. In the restaurant industry there are definitely a few processes that you have to go through if you are going to succeed. When you are starting a new restaurant, the PR machine is the most important thing, and that should kick in about three or four months before your planned opening. Once you are in the PR phase you need to make sure that everything you say to a journalist, every photograph that goes out, every article you do – you have to make sure you deliver, right from day one. For example, with the relaunch of the Blackheath site as a Loco restaurant, I deliberately didn't go round saying, 'Oh this is on the back of my TV series with Giorgio Locatelli, so it's going to be the best Italian restaurant you will eat in.' Instead we kept it very low key, so that when people came in they had reasonable expectations, which we were able to exceed – and that kept them coming back again.

It is all about matching the PR to the kind of restaurant you are aiming to end up with. When we opened Bank we were aiming at the very top, and the PR hype had to match that. We wanted to be talked about, because we were confident we could deliver the experience that all the publicity was promising, and of course, we did. When we opened the Guildford branch of Fish!, we did a lot of publicity for the setting, because it is genuinely different and dramatic. But you can't do that sort of thing if there's no basis in fact – over-hype can ruin a restaurant. You see it all the time, especially with a restaurant that's dependent on a star name. At the end of the day even the most fashionable, best-looking chef in the world can't reinvent the wheel. His spaghetti Arabiata's not going to be that different from what you can get in your local neighbourhood Italian eatery, so there's no point pretending it is.

It is a similar situation with the pricing of your menu. I firmly believe that you shouldn't start cheap and then price up as the restaurant becomes more popular. I think you should start at the price you want to charge the customer in the long term, otherwise they will feel ripped off when they come back. But the amount of people I see opening restaurants and bars and getting bums on seats and then start edging the prices up, that's a formula for disaster, and there's a lot of restaurants gone by the wayside because of that. I'm still arguing about that even now over the pricing of Fish! Kitchen. A lot of chef/patrons don't have a very good grounding in what I would call business common sense. You get a very good cook who thinks it's a good idea to open a restaurant, and they forget that it's a business as well. You know, there are some real fundamentals that apply in our industry just like any other. If something is worth a pound, as a businessman you want to pay 25p for it, not 50p, not 75p and certainly not a pound. Then you want to find out who it's worth a pound to, and sell it to him – and that holds good whatever trade you are in.

Food is in many ways just like any other raw material, in that you make your profit by adding value. It's a given that you buy it for as little as possible, and then you make it worth as much as possible. Pricing isn't the only way you do that. For a start you try to make your operation as efficient as possible. How you are efficient can vary from restaurant to restaurant. At Bank restaurant we were looking at an upmarket venue so we could afford to high end it, even to the extent of slightly over-staffing in order to get the very slick, smooth image we wanted to present. With Fish! we took a different angle and made the whole operation very low-cost so that we were still highly profitable even though our margins were lower. But even when you have planned which way you want to go, you should try to be as flexible as possible, because you can't always predict how a restaurant will develop. When I open a new restaurant I will always give an element of leeway at first. I'll give the chef and the restaurant manager anything between six to eight weeks before I start looking at their profit lines. It's very positive to be able to have the luxury of time and staff while you are first getting the formula correct first. Then you can chuck the costs into place.

If I was explaining all this to a group of MBA students I imagine there are scientific formulas and statistics you could use to describe it, but really there's no need to over-complicate. Essentially what I have done is very simple. I had a good, innovative idea which filled a gap in the market place. I identified the right people, not only to do the job, but who could work with me. I didn't rush to expand initially, and equally importantly I didn't get myself too knotted up with the whole idea of being a businessman. One of the most difficult things as you get bigger is not to lose sight of the customer. The truism that the customer is always right does hold good – you have to provide what the people want first and foremost. The only times where I have been in danger of losing my touch are when I've moved away from that. A huge business strength for me had been my upbringing, where I live (and have basically always lived), the fact that I am a suburban man. I know what the grass roots people of this country want because I'm one of them.

I think that's worked in my favour in a lot of different ways, in my personal life as well as business. It helps you to stay grounded when life gets tough. Because one of things you have to come to terms with when eventually you do make it is that you are going to experience a certain amount of envy and resentment directed towards you. Even people who are close to you can get chippy about it. It is quite a British thing, I think, that we don't really respect entrepreneurial success in the way that say, the Americans do. You get no praise when you're successful in this country. And you would be surprised at where the antagonism comes from. I remember winning Entrepreneur of the Year, and I was walking back from the stage to go back to my table and this guy half rose from his seat and muttered, 'Oh, well done', and in the next breath he said, 'That's the kiss of death that award, you know. Everybody that's won that award has gone down the pan.' I thought to myself, he's sitting there, basking in my success and me paying him fifty thousand pounds a year – and that's the best he can do?

Nor is it just business colleagues and friends who can be negative. When one member of the family makes it in a big way, it can be very difficult for the rest of the family, to the point where you can have serious fallings out. Particularly in my case, where I have employed the majority of my immediate family at one time or another, it can be very much a two-edged sword. At one stage I fell out with my father because of various things that were written about me in the press, and my relationship with my brother has been very up and down. One of the worst things was when one of the more distant family members who worked for me was caught with his hands in the till – something which people have since told me is inevitable at one time or another. But it is still very difficult to deal with, and that's when you see the family all fall apart. My experience of that was that for three years I didn't speak to that part of the family because everybody was taking sides about what had happened. Even so, I'm a big advocate of having my family working for me, I always have been. My mum has always been a really valued member of the team in one role or another, and Denys gets more involved now as the children are growing up. And even though it hasn't always been easy for me and my brother, I am still the first to say that he did a great job for me at Cutty's. He's in Dubai now doing his own thing, and I wish him well. But you have to realize that it can be very frustrating for family members to stand by and watch another person's star rising. For a long time I just wouldn't think about those things – that friends, family, parents even, could be jealous. I think I was in denial about that aspect of success, but you come to terms with it in the end. And where I have been very lucky is that in my home life, with Denys and the girls, we have all kept our feet on the ground.

The most important things in my life are Denys and the kids, Charlie and Holly. We have been very lucky with the girls; they are growing up to be such great people. Holly reminds me a lot of Denys. She's very bright, and all set on being an architect. I'm thrilled about it because I think she was actually inspired to get interested in design and architecture by what Julian Wickham did with Bank – the chandelier and everything. This is the moment when you realize why you've done it all, because the money is meaningless in itself, it's what you can do with your position that counts. And luckily, through business I have made some great contacts in architecture which I hope will be a help to her if she does go into it as a career. It's extraordinary to me – it will be builder to architect in three generations! Holly, our younger daughter, is the flamboyant one. She reminds me of me quite a lot – always doing three things at once. I'm pretty sure both the girls will stay level-headed. We've tried not to spoil them too much, and to give them a sense of the value of money. With Charlie for example, we gave her a nice car when she learned to drive, but at the same time she works in the Blackheath restaurant two nights a week to earn her allowance. Charlie gets a lot of pleasure out of achieving things, getting things done, being organized, so I'm not worried about her. She'll probably get a flat from us when she's ready – but as long as she works I don't mind that she might get a few treats. Whereas having that same philosophy with Holly may be a little bit trickier. Holly is so naturally gifted at pretty much everything she does that her sheer talent may make things a bit too easy for her. But I know she will achieve whatever she wants!

Denys gave up work when we had Charlie, and concentrated on raising the girls and providing the home support which was so valuable to me over the years. Luckily she had her extended family to help. Her parents lived nearby and adored helping with their first grandchild, which was important for Denys because you have to remember that I was hardly ever at home during that period. Working an average 16-hour day, I really only ever got home to see the children go to bed and grab a couple of hours sleep myself. It definitely was no picnic for Denys with two young daughters and a husband involved in all these huge – and sometimes risky – business projects. I think we're very lucky in one respect that none of us is depressive, and we have a fantastic relationship. Like any couple, we've had our ups and downs. We did go through the classic seven-year-itch phase. It would have been in about 1993, not long after Holly was born, and we just started falling out for no real reason. I suppose I was being selfish. I was very bound up in work at the time and when I came home all I wanted to do was sleep, but I felt as if I was being nagged. We had a sticky year, and I ended up going and getting a flat somewhere at one stage because I thought they were all against me. I think partly the difficulties, for Denys, was having just had our second child. She wanted to get her figure back and everything and I think mums can lose a bit of confidence about being themselves rather than just a mother. And there I was, driving an open-topped Porsche with my hair and my leather jacket, and every time I went into a restaurant, some girl would flutter her eyelids – which was something Denys didn't take kindly to. She's always been, not exactly possessive, but pretty firm about 'that's my husband'.

I was high profile within the restaurant industry, while Denys was probably at a low ebb, so there were a few rows and I ended up going over to Europe to visit our French and Spanish suppliers. It was over the August bank holiday, and we were supposed to be on a family holiday, and there I was in Spain. I was away on my own for the first time ever almost and the first couple of days were great, I was having a laugh. Then it suddenly hit me: I should be at home; I should be with Denys and the kids. It brought me back to my senses and I went straight home, got my stuff out of the flat, and went back to being a fishmonger again. It wasn't so much that we changed how we did things as a couple after that, but it was a shock to the system for us both. We had that time away from each other – even though it was only about six weeks – and we discovered it was something we'd never wanted in the first place. And that was probably the first time ever, I just said 'bollocks to it', and I realized I had to start delegating a bit more.

Because you couldn't want for a better wife than Denys. Her timing is impeccable. She knows when to get me in a good moment. Or if it's a bad moment, she's very diplomatic. She's always been very caring. And one of the things I value most is that she's always had the utmost faith in me and everything I have done. That support has been so tremendous to have during my working life. At one stage I had over 1000 staff, and Denys would get frustrated because I put myself in place 1001. She would encourage me to create a bit more time for myself. I think now I'm finally beginning to see it her way, and I think the moment is right for me to spend more time enjoying my home life with Denys and Charlie and Holly.

It was really only a few years ago that I finally began to learn how to relax. From the time after the court case I started to question how things were going, and that's when I went away and discovered the virtue of spoiling yourself occasionally. I have started watching sport again, which is something I really enjoy. I love my football and cricket, and I had missed out on more or less a whole decade of it. I think I have gradually realized that you can burn yourself out, and now that I have begun to let go a bit, it is as if a wave of tension has been realized that has probably been there underneath for more than 20 years. A lot of top businessmen talk about how important it is to have balance in your life, and at last I understand what they mean! You feel like a puppet with someone always pulling the strings, and when you actually turn around and say 'to hell with it', it's the most liberating experience. And it's not something I want to lose sight of, so I'm going to make sure over the next couple of years that I don't fall back into that very driven place.

For one thing, I'm going to go fishing! I have always loved coarse fishing. The other day I was fishing on the Thames, right underneath the Dartford Bridge, and I actually managed to catch six sea bass. What a great feeling to have risen to the challenge of catching good fish in the Thames itself. I want to start learning to fly fish as well. But I think my favourite is pike fishing. There are some great pike lakes I go to at Darenth and near Woking. It's always best to set up while it is still dark. So I get my rods out in the early hours of the morning and get to the lake before dawn. You are sitting there by the water as the sun comes up, and the mist gradually clears from the reeds and there is nobody there but you and the wildlife. That's a wonderful sensation that has nothing really to do with catching fish and everything to do with getting away from the manic PR-driven world that normally surrounds you. I always used to find relaxing very difficult, but sports like fishing and shooting have given an extra dimension to my life. Shooting especially takes you to an amazing place. You can get on such a high, it really affects you. But work spoils it! If I had it my way though, would I give up work completely? I'm lucky enough to be in the position where that isn't out of the question. Yet here I am still opening restaurants, still launching new projects, so there must be something I'm enjoying. Basically, work does spoil it – but if you can treat your job like you do your hobbies, that is the way to do it.

Appendix

TONY ALLAN –
the Key Dates

1964 – born in Erith, North Kent. Brought up in neighbouring Sidcup and Bexleyheath. A schoolboy rebel.

1979 – attends catering college at SE London Technical College, Lewisham, where he discovers his talent as a chef.

1981 – first employment in the industry as a junior chef at Claridges, Mayfair.

1982 – moves to The Dorchester to work under exciting new head chef, Anton Mossiman.

1983 – first senior kitchen appointment as sous chef at Corney and Barrow, Moorgate.

1984 – first head chef role at Salters Court, Covent Garden aged only 20, but sacked by the end of the year.

1985 – starts a self-employed business buying and selling fresh fish, called Cutty's.

1995 – ten years later Cutty's has grown to a £12 million turnover business, with £1 million annual profit.

1996 – borrows money to launch Bank restaurant at Aldwych in London, rapidly named restaurant of the year by *The Times*.

1997 – Bank wins best newcomer award.

1998 – Bank Group Restaurants floated on the AIM with an initial capitalization of £46 million, rapidly growing to £80 million. Tony Allan wins AIM Entrepreneur of the Year. Marco Pierre White commences a libel action against Tony Allan.

1999 – Opens Fish! restaurant at Borough Market, at the southern end of London Bridge.

2001 – BGR sells Bank, Bank Birmingham and Zander to a newly formed Bank Restaurant Group for £11 million. A new company Fish! is founded with Tony Allan as chairman. Fish! rapidly expands to a chain of 20 restaurants. Libel case with Marco Pierre White reaches the High Court and Tony settles out of court for £1 million.

May 2002 – Fish! issues profits warning.

June 2002 – Fish! appoints administrators.

August 2002 – Tony buys back seven Fish! restaurants from the administrators, then sells three of them.

2003 – BBC screens *Tony & Giorgio* cookery series, with Giorgio Locatelli. Tony launches Loco Locale. Relaunches Fish! Borough Market.

2004 – Opens Loco Locale in Fulham, London.

2005 – Opens Fish! Kitchen in Kingston-upon-Thames.

Index